T0243926

A NOTE ON THE AUTHOR

Dr. Olivia Remes is a mental health researcher at the University of Cambridge, a public speaker and a life coach. Her previous book, *The Instant Mood Fix*, was sold in 23 countries around the world. Dr. Olivia Remes has researched mental health and wellbeing for over a decade, and her work has been featured by the BBC, National Public Radio (NPR) in the U.S., the *Times of India*, and Channel News Asia. She has written for *Vogue* magazine, is a regular speaker on BBC Cambridgeshire Radio (Wellbeing Wednesday) and her TED Talks have garnered more than 6 million views combined.

THIS IS HOW YOU GROW AFTER TRAUMA

SIMPLE STRATEGIES FOR RESILIENCE, CONFIDENCE, HEALING & HOPE

DR OLIVIA REMES

Published by Sourcebooks
P.O. Box 4410, Naperville, Illinois 60567-4410
(630) 961-3900
sourcebooks.com

Originally published in 2023 in Great Britain by Ebury Press, an imprint of
Ebury Publishing. Ebury Press is part of the Penguin Random House group of
companies whose addresses can be found at global.penguinrandomhouse.com

Cataloging-in-Publication Data is on file with the Library of Congress.

Printed and bound in the United States of America.
MA 10 9 8 7 6 5 4 3 2 1

I dedicate this book to my mom.

CONTENTS

ABOUT THIS BOOK

Over the past decade at the University of Cambridge, I have researched the science of wellbeing and growing after difficulties. I have interviewed and spoken with hundreds of people about tough circumstances they've dealt with and how they bounced back. My research and own pursuit of the science of growth has led me to scour the academic literature and read hundreds of studies. I have taken the work I've done over the past decade, and retained the key, essential aspects on growing after life's difficulties and now I share them with you.

This book is for anyone who has experienced a tough time including trauma, and my aim is that it gives you the tools you need to move forward. It shows how you can become a more confident, self-reliant and stronger person in spite of difficulties. And bounce back.

One day, as I was working, I stumbled upon an article that would change the trajectory I would take - and my life. The article talked about how people who were going through tough times - an illness, an accident, a loss, a devastating break-up or job loss - had *grown* because of their experience. These people were experiencing distress, but at the same time, they were transforming. They were in pain, but profound changes were taking place within them *at the same time*. Over the following years, I discovered a treasure trove: hundreds of studies that had been written along the years on this kind of growth, but that didn't quite make it into the public domain. And yet, it gave you so much hope when you read about it.

This book is about a profound change, a wake-up call that makes you realize what your life priorities are. It's the ice bucket that wakes you up from the deep sleep that so many of us are in as we go through life. I found myself thinking: 'What if everyone knew this?'

When you go through something difficult, the crisis you're in can wake you up to what is important. You start to become more open to experiences in life. You start to perceive new possibilities, realize that you need people more than you thought, and develop a new appreciation for life that might not have been there before the difficulty. When I wrote an article about this for *Vogue*, it was published across the globe. I noticed that people from all over the world want to know that 'hope is scientifically proven to exist',[1] and that we can bounce back from difficulties and trauma. And we can.

Not only this, but even in the most difficult of times, there are people who seem to thrive in the midst of change, while others spiral downwards. Some people who face major stressful upheavals are able to retain their health, while others don't. So why do some manage better than others? The difference seems to lie in a key set of inner strengths that can be developed. We will look at those in this book, among other key aspects.

I wanted to take the research and interviews I conducted and help people heal from difficulties they've experienced. And so, I wrote this book. I wrote this book to help people find the first ray of light again, and to help them realize what steps to take to GROW.

In this book we're not taking a light-hearted approach to difficulties. Not at all. Facing life problems can be hard. It can affect your mental health and increase the risk for anxiety and depression. When you experience serious issues, such as receiving devastating personal news, are subjected to bullying or face a relationship hurdle that can leave you traumatized, you may become despondent. You might start getting intrusive thoughts about what what's happened. So dealing with a crisis or shock is hard. But while you're trying to become adjusted to this new grim reality, you also grow.

We are going to look at:

Tough times and trauma I'm going to show you inner strengths that help you bounce back from trauma and tough challenges. This will help you feel in charge of your life again.

Gratitude I will tell you exactly why gratitude is important, and how to develop a new appreciation for life.

Relationships We'll look at how to create connections with other people and how to create a stronger relationship with yourself.

Resilience If one area of your life isn't going well (for example, your work or personal life), I will share with you something you can do right now, so that you can still feel good about yourself.

Mindsets I will share with you how you can beat thinking patterns that sabotage you, and antidotes to toxic thinking.

Motivation and persistence If you're going through a tough time or are in a slump, this can make it easier to indulge in unwanted behaviours or bad habits. We will look at how to beat the behaviours holding you back, and develop motivation and persistence to reach your goals.

The core of the book is divided into the following four parts:

G - Gratitude
R - Relationships & Resilience
O - Openness
W - Waking up

Each of these parts has two chapters dedicated to it. The first chapter sets the scene and talks about the science or background behind the topic. The second chapter presents strategies and exercises: some of these are very practical in nature, while others are more subtle and help to increase self-awareness. The second chapter starts off with emergency strategies that can help you straight away if you're dealing with a difficulty or crisis. The longer-term coping strategies form part of your long-term plan going forward. This book is based on research and contains real stories.[1-112]

If you've been trying strategies up until now to get closer to the life you want but it hasn't worked, let's wipe the slate clean and start over. Put away the books, articles and everything else that isn't helping you get to where you want to, and let me show you a new way.

Let's get started.

CHAPTER 1

WHAT IS TRAUMA AND HOW CAN WE BOUNCE BACK FROM IT?

In order to best learn how to grow after encountering difficulties in life or traumatic situations, let's first take a look at what trauma is.

Trauma is an emotional response to something difficult that has happened in your life. Maybe you experienced a devastating break-up, a job loss, an accident or abuse. Or maybe you've had a difficult upbringing. These experiences can be traumatic and they can affect your mental and physical health.

Reactions to trauma

In the short-term, your reaction to the traumatic event can be shock and denial. You can't believe what has just taken place. And you might be in denial about what's happened. When your world has shattered, this can be stressful and so, turning to denial can give you a sense of protection: you're avoiding the overwhelming stress and crisis. Therefore, denial can be a way of coping with the crisis. In the long-term however, being in a state of denial can make it difficult to adjust.

TRAUMA CAN AFFECT YOUR WORLDVIEW

Many times, we assume that life is fair or predictable. We presume that we'll reach old age or that if we do good deeds, we'll be rewarded. And when something happens that directly contradicts these assumptions or beliefs, it can be traumatic. We all tend to have a worldview, which consists of our attitudes about life. When a crisis or shock takes place and we're presented with a new reality - a frightful new world which we haven't inhabited before, which is in stark contrast to our worldview - this can be traumatic. And we react. We may get physical symptoms, flashbacks and nightmares.

Despite this, one of the main things that research on trauma offers to us is hope: the hope that you can transition from being a victim of trauma - someone who may find it difficult to take steps forward and feels discouraged - to a 'mobile survivor'[2] who has bounced back. Someone who has shifted from a state of potential helplessness to an active state - a state in which you're not only accepting what has happened, but adapting to a new life.[2] And even flourishing. This book will show you the path towards this.

THE STEELING EFFECT

Studies have shown that stressful or adverse experiences can have a steeling effect. Namely, facing challenges could actually be beneficial; you can develop a steel-like strength in you that can shield you from stress. This was seen in children who had to take on adult roles during the Great Depression - it was a hard time and people faced poverty, but despite this, the children who took on extra responsibilities showed greater psychological strengths later. Hardship is tough to endure, but it can teach people coping strategies and contribute to an internal toughness. So even though we may fear obstacles in life, they can indeed make us stronger.

STRENGTHS THAT HELP YOU BOUNCE BACK

When researchers looked at the effects of trauma decades ago, they predominantly looked at the negative - how trauma led to depression and posttraumatic stress disorder, among other things. In one of my articles, I wrote that, 'When we're going through tough times . . . or if you suffer from anxiety or depression, for example, or find out that you've got an illness, you tend to hear about how bad it is and how you spiral downwards. But what is usually not talked about is how we can actually grow stronger from hardship and obstacles.'[1] This isn't about positive thinking with no basis to it. This is about understanding human nature and our capacity to rise back up after we fall down. And this can give way to hope and the belief that out of great tragedy, great strength arises.

In more recent times, researchers realized that it can be incredibly insightful to also focus on those who remain healthy in spite of negative experiences. Instead of researching primarily those aspects related to impairment, they decided to also study the people who retained their wellbeing. This gave way to thinking that tough times could have beneficial effects. And that they could help us grow psychologically.

STRESS AND TRAUMA

What is stress? Stress is that feeling you typically get when you're under pressure or feel alarmed. In our lives, we may experience events that can give rise to stress and make us feel traumatized.

If you are dealing with a stressful, difficult life problem at the moment, such as a condition you're suffering from, or if you're under the threat of violence at home, or you lost your job - this can be incredibly hard. If you're faced with hardships like this, is there a way out? One of the ways is hardiness.

Hardiness

Years back, I came across a study on high stress by Suzanne Kobasa, which she wrote in 1979.[4] It was the foundational study that introduced the concept of hardiness to the world. Hardiness is the combination of personal strengths that can help you when you're faced with traumatic, stressful situations. And you can learn the skills for these strengths.

Suzanne Kobasa studied middle- and upper-level executives who had been exposed to high levels of stressful life events in the past three years. Some of these executives were able to remain healthy despite the high stress, while others became sick. The ones who *didn't* fall ill appeared to be protected by this internal resource (a combination of strengths) called hardiness. People with this internal resource tended to have a commitment to life, they had 'an attitude of vigorousness' and 'a sense of meaningfulness' in life; they believed they were in control and that their own actions could make a difference.[4] These inner strengths, it seems, protected them from falling ill when faced with high stress.

In 2018, I became interested in the concept of hardiness. The study I was using at the University of Cambridge was an inspiration for me and it kick-started my interest in this concept. The study at Cambridge started in the early 1990s and looked at the health and lifestyle of over 30,000 participants. It measured a number of aspects, including hardiness. To understand more about the study, I visited the mobile clinic where participants went to get their measurements taken in Norwich, England. And I collaborated and wrote papers with the researchers who started this study.

ARE YOU HARDY?

Hardy people are those who don't lose sight of their values and goals, even when the going gets tough. They remain actively involved in life and what's going on around them instead of reacting with passivity. If they must transfer to another job or move to a new place, hardy people think about how they can make it work: for example, getting involved in community activities or learning skills in the new role that can help their career. Even though they have little to no control over a circumstance - such as having to work with a co-worker they don't like - the hardy person decides how they want to approach the situation instead of seeing themselves as powerless. So instead of avoiding the co-worker, avoiding the work, or distracting themselves from the stressful situation by turning to alcohol or other unhealthy habits, the hardy person thinks about how they can problem-solve. They think about how hey can keep their eye on the goal and move forward.[4-5]

Work by other scientists showed that hardiness had a substantial effect on people, and I wanted to find out more. Hardiness seemed to be a key element when it comes to growth and recovery in spite of hardship. And it is an important concept in the context of trauma. Hardiness is made up of three aspects:

1. Commitment
2. Control
3. Challenge

Commitment refers to having a curiosity about the world and involving yourself in life's activities. You believe that life is meaningful. **Control** refers to believing in your ability to influence the course of your life, and **challenge** refers to accepting that life is ever-changing but that this change and unpredictability is exactly what contributes to our own development. Change is a normal part of life and can be a stimulus for our growth.

These are the 3 Cs of hardiness.[3] When people go through tough times, embodying these three aspects can help us.

A landmark study on people who had encountered significant difficulties at work in the 1980s shed much light on hardiness. In 1981, the Illinois Bell Telephone Company underwent significant downsizing. In just one year, it eliminated over half of its original workforce. It had approximately 26,000 employees in 1981 and downsized to about 14,000 in 1982. In a very short time, all sorts of changes were made to the company's goals, leadership personnel and staff job roles. For one manager, the change resulted in him having 12 different supervisors in the timespan of one year. Chaos seemed to pervade.[5]

A study was done on personnel from this company, and the researcher behind this study was Dr. Salvatore Maddi from the University of Chicago. He assessed staff before, during and after the downsizing took place, and so he was able to track health-related factors at different stages of the process, among other aspects.[6]

Whenever rapid change takes place, this can overwhelm the body and mind - it may place a tremendous burden on people's coping capacities and lead to a downward spiral. And this is exactly what happened to the staff of this telephone company. The downsizing and significant stresses that people were subjected to were linked to heart attacks, depression, substance abuse and divorces.

However, one-third of the group studied actually ended up doing quite well, despite the disruption and stressful change. In fact, they thrived in the face of the challenges. Some of these people who remained at the company rose to the top; others who left started their own ventures or became involved with newly established businesses and excelled in that arena. These people not only managed to pull through during a highly stressful time, but showed psychological growth.[5]

Dr. Maddi has done a substantial amount of work on hardiness. Through his work, we now have a greater understanding of hardiness. Instead of perceiving a negative situation as something that can bring us down, we realize that it's a core part of life. We can view it as a challenge that can help us grow. It's about finding the meaning in the adversity and strengthening our skills to view key problems in life differently.

Dr. Maddi's research and legacy carry on. Staff have been trained to become hardier in various organizations and it has spread to the military. Students have been taught this concept in various educational settings. The work on hardiness has pervaded society and paved the way for the wellbeing movement. Many of the things you know about positive psychology and this focus on the positive emerged in part because of the work done by researcher and professor Dr. Maddi. The Dean of the School of Social Ecology at the University of Chicago, where Dr. Maddi was based, says that this researcher was an 'insightful scientist who cared deeply about understanding ways that stressful or traumatic experiences could be catalysts for growth'.[7]

HARDINESS AND TRAUMA

So how are hardiness and trauma connected? Hardiness is linked to helpful coping strategies and, in this way, can serve as a buffer against highly stressful or traumatic experiences. Hardiness also stimulates people to seek help from others. And seeking help and getting support is really important when we are going through tough times. In fact, research on war veterans has shown that those who display the three characteristics of hardiness - who exhibit this sense of control over their lives, have a commitment to finding meaning for their lives and are open to seeing change as a challenge - have fewer posttraumatic stress disorder symptoms.[8]

Hardy people are more likely to spot and seek help from those around them during tough, stressful times.

Hardy people find it easier to identify the necessary support[8] and find ways to be embedded in supportive networks. Being part of social networks and having friends and family around you when you're going through a tough time is incredibly helpful. Social support can serve as a buffer against the negative effects of stressful and potentially damaging experiences. In this way, hardiness can be a key factor in the adjustment of people who have been exposed to trauma.

How does hardiness work?

It is thought that hardiness allows people to face adversity and, at the same time, reframe the difficulty. Reframing means that instead of seeing the stressful circumstance as something to be feared, you see it in a more positive, helpful way. Perhaps the stressful event is something that can give you insights for your life and shape you in new ways. In contrast, if you're not hardy, then you're more likely to see the stressful event in a negative light, which can stand in the way of you looking for options or a way out of the turmoil.[3]

Hardiness allows people to move away from the rumination related to the traumatic event. Rather, it allows you to focus on the benefits of what you've experienced and find some sort of meaning in it all. Even if it's hard to find a meaning for your suffering, when you try to think of what you've gained from your experience, it can make it easier to go through this world. And it can make it easier to believe that the world is still a good place.[3]

When severely injured military personnel who had lost limbs were surveyed along with their spouses, hardy participants showed growth after trauma. Even in such devastating circumstances, hardy individuals were able to identify benefits that arose out of the traumatic situation: for example, they became more resilient and developed deeper connections with their loved ones.[3-9]

People who are hardy are more likely to re-interpret the hardship in a way that is positive. They turn the difficulty into a chance for growth. Recovery is perceived as a possibility.[3]

Hardiness may also stimulate active coping - you're actively involved with your circumstance in order to alter it. When you're actively coping, you're taking steps to bounce back or steps to avoid being in a similar situation in the future.[3] For example, a man who is diagnosed with liver problems because he has been drinking for far too long starts taking active steps to get out of the situation - this is active coping, he's not passive. He joins an Alcoholics Anonymous group and finds an accountability buddy to help him stick to his goals. He also thinks of ways to prevent future liver problems.

This is in contrast to being passive or avoiding the problem. It's the opposite of denying or refusing to acknowledge the issue. People who aren't hardy are more likely to avoid tackling the problem that's in front of them, and this can increase their risk of depression.[3-10-11] In contrast, when you see yourself as an active agent in your life and are actively coping with the obstacles that come your way, this can make you feel in control again. And this feeling of control is part of hardiness.

Hardiness and stress

So far, we've talked about high stress, such as that found in Dr. Maddi's study. However, the studies on hardiness can inspire us even when we're dealing with lower levels of stress. If we're not feeling as committed to life, if we don't feel fully in control of our lives, we can start by asking ourselves: what is the first next step you can take? How can you develop these inner strengths? This can help us so that if we ever do encounter more extreme stress, we will be better prepared.

There can be moderate or milder levels of stress that we experience on a day-to-day basis, which can negatively affect our wellbeing - for example, the stress before a presentation or a deadline. Stress pervades our society and can have different effects on people. Our modern way of life is fast, we are multi-tasking, and more often than not, people are feeling overwhelmed: the to-do lists, the constant stream of emails, the need to find and keep a job - all of this can make us feel like we're in a never-ending race. It can make us feel fatigued and sometimes we can't keep up anymore.

In fact, stress happens when our internal resources don't match the demands from the external environment.[12-13] When we don't have what it takes anymore to keep up with the never-ending demands of the day, and we are thrown off balance. But if we turn to hardiness, and practise developing the 3 Cs of hardiness – challenge, control and commitment – we often begin to fare better. We begin to keep up and maybe even feel less stressed. Let's take a look to see how we can tackle stress through the 3 Cs of hardiness.

Challenge

One of these three Cs is **challenge**. So instead of seeing the stressor as a threat, as something that provokes anxiety, let's practise seeing it as a challenge. It's all in how you see things: how you perceive the world around you.

Threats can be linked to anxiety and make us afraid to take action, so if you perceive a setback as a threat, this can be a major roadblock. But perceiving something as a challenge is much more positive – it's stimulating. And when you take the first step forward (and reframe the obstacle as a potentially worthy challenge instead of a threat), your stress levels can go down. When you see something as a challenge, you're more motivated to act. It can stimulate personal growth.[12]

Even though it's stressful, is there anything you can learn from this? Can you grow from this experience?

This changes our perception from negative to positive, and we become more willing to tackle the stressor or difficult situation. The dictionary states that challenge is something that 'requires great effort and determination'.[14] The first key word is *effort*. And the second key word is determination: having a willingness to keep going until you reach your goal. It's not about how smart you are or the abilities you were born with – it's about the effort you put in. This reminds me of the research on the growth mindset.[15] When people are in the growth mindset, they relish the challenge of tackling a difficult or complex situation. In the growth mindset, *not* succeeding when faced with a difficult situation isn't seen as failure; perceived mistakes aren't an opportunity to beat yourself up over them. Rather, failure becomes a learning opportunity, a chance to try out a new strategy. People with a growth mindset are more likely to believe that effort is a key ingredient linked to their development.[15] This can have an impact on personal success and outcomes in life.

When we perceive that we can change our outcomes in life by the effort we put in, we start to feel that things are within our control. And this can give us a feeling of motivation. So perceiving something as a challenge is part of hardiness and this can help us move forward.

Changing how you see life's challenges
People may struggle with the challenges that deal with significant life changes: the move to a new place, changing job, the transition to singlehood after a relationship ends, dealing with a new reality following a setback.

Challenge, as a construct of hardiness, can be characterized as the belief that change is normal and often required for our own growth. So if you're hardy, you're more likely to see change as an aspect that is just part of life, it can even be something positive that helps you evolve. In this way, change can be a 'stimulus to enhance maturity rather than a threat to security'.[12] Instead of seeing change as something fearful, you're more likely to see it as something that can help you grow. Instead of assuming that life will run predictably and smoothly, you realize that stressful times can sometimes come your way. This is part of the natural ebb and flow of life, and going through difficulties can help you develop into a wiser being. We often want stability in life, but the reality is that it's ever-changing.[16] As the Greek philosopher Heraclitus said, *the only constant in life is change.*

Sometimes we see change as threatening and we fear novelty. For example, Jessica, a mechanical engineer that I coach, had just stopped working for a firm she had been with for six years. Not only did she have to find a new job but also a place to live. The prospect of moving out of her current place was daunting to her. The idea of looking for a new place and moving out all the stuff she had accumulated over the years was overwhelming. She looked to the near future with dread. But when we started talking about hardiness and how science suggests that change can be an opportunity; it's 'a stimulus to enhance maturity rather than a threat to security',[12] she began to see the move and job change as a necessary shift for her self-growth. And the stress went down.

Control

In my coaching session with Jessica, we also talked about control, which is another 'C' of hardiness. Feeling in control is the opposite of feeling helpless. Perhaps you've faced adversity, but you recognize that there may be actions that you can take to help you recover.[3]

When you're in control, you're in the driver's seat and decide where you go. Reflecting on this helped Jessica deal with the stress, and we brainstormed small things she could do each day to make her feel in greater control of her life. Some of these were small, simple things like eating breakfast first thing in the morning and going to the gym to feel energized throughout the day. Reflecting on ways she could become an active agent in her life - rather than a passive observer - and taking active steps helped her feel that she was deciding the direction of her life.

Commitment

And finally, we devised a plan to keep Jessica actively involved in her life's journey, even when the going got tough. We talked about ways that she can persevere and remain committed to her plan even if there were bumps in the road, which is also part of hardiness. She realized that she needed to remain an active participant of life, no matter how bad things got, rather than become detached from the world.[16]

One of the things I suggested included making a list of the goals that stimulated her, the steps she would take each week to meet these goals, and I encouraged her to find an accountability system to keep her on track (e.g. an accountability buddy that she could check in with). We practised changing the way she saw her goals: instead of perceiving them as difficult or hard to reach, we focused on the benefits of taking active steps. We focused on her desire to succeed in her new job and interest in learning something new.

When you practise seeing threats as challenges, commit to life and your goals and find ways to stay in control, this helps you tap into the inner resource of hardiness.

Conclusion

When people are faced with adversity or trauma, this can have a significant negative effect on their wellbeing. This chapter has shown the strengths that can help people bounce back from trauma or life difficulties. We can keep in mind the three Cs - challenge, control and commitment, and develop these internal resources to help us manage when the going gets tough.

CHAPTER 2

GRATITUDE: THE SCIENCE BEHIND THIS

Even if you haven't gone through great difficulties in life, reading about those who have and how they bounced back can be inspiring. It can make us less afraid. Less afraid of life's ups and downs, and the uncontrollability of life. Aaron Antonovsky, the great scientist, talked about the chaotic, ever-changing life we're living in. And how we can manage it.

Here is the science and real stories of people who went through some of the hardest times and grew psychologically. **Appreciation or gratitude is at the core of this**.

MY STORY

I would like to share with you how gratitude entered my life after experiencing something rather traumatic that dented my life. I still think about this every so often, and the memory of that experience brings up feelings of gratitude that I am now able to eat and sleep. And lead a mostly routine life without my body surprising me in distressing, unpleasant ways.

I had always struggled with stomach problems and allergies, but one day in May, several years ago, I realized that I wasn't able to eat *anything* anymore without developing painful, burning welts all over my body. Even the most basic vegetable or simple rice dishes would cause a reaction as soon as I ate them. Even allergy medication would make me react. The nights were the worst because this was when the welts would appear all over my body, and they would wake me up. They were like giant, raised, red spider bites all over my skin, and it was painful to even just lie down in bed. My face would regularly swell up: my lips would swell sometimes to twice the size of their usual thickness. I lost a lot of weight, some of my hair fell out, and I felt so weak and low on energy that I missed months of work.

Needless to say, any glimmer of happiness was gone and I just tried to make it through each day. This lasted for about a year, and it took months and months of carefully reintroducing food into my diet that helped me get better. I never bounced back to the mostly allergy-free state I had previously been in, but after a year, my body learned to tolerate a handful of food products.

The only food item I didn't react to in the beginning phase of that awful time was peas. Now, when I eat peas, they bring back memories of having lunch with the people at work: all of us around the lunch table, and everyone eating sandwiches, pasta dishes, hot soup, while I'd be eating peas. I remember bringing a large clear glass container to work that would be filled with peas. And each time a someone new joined the group, I had to explain my situation all over again. But it wasn't always tough times. Whenever I was able to introduce a new food item, there'd be celebration in our little group. Clare would exclaim, 'You're able to eat a new thing now!' and that brief moment of gratitude and celebration stayed with me.

This extremely difficult experience changed me and made me see things differently. Going through this made me become grateful for even the smallest joys in life: being able to eat an apple or have a treat once in a while without having my body break out into hives or having my face swell up. Or being able to sleep through the night (even if I didn't necessarily feel energized the next day). It made me go back to basics and appreciate life at its core - in its simplicity:

being able to eat, sleep and go for a walk without being in pain. Ironically, after this horrible year was over, this is also when I developed a sense of peace I never quite had before. And the gratitude for the small joys in life hasn't left me. You could say, it permanently changed me.

GRATITUDE AND WELLBEING

Gratitude can emerge on its own: maybe you experience a shock, a health crisis or devastating personal news, and after some time, you develop a new appreciation for life. But gratitude can also be called forth through the things that we do, such as taking some time out of our day to think over the little things that make us feel thankful, such as a nice family dinner or feeling better lately.

What we clearly know from research is that gratitude has a real impact on our wellbeing. This was one of the key findings from research led by the Federal University of Health Sciences of Porto Alegre, which examined over 400 participants. Here's how it unfolded.

The experimenters divided the participants into three groups. The people in the study would use 10-20 minutes before bedtime to write about five things that had occurred to them over the past day. But the things they wrote about varied depending on the group they were in:

- *The Gratitude Group*: these participants were asked to write about five things they'd been grateful for over the past day.
- *The Hassles Group*: people in this group were instructed to note down five situations that had irritated or annoyed them over the past day.

- *The Neutral Events Group*: here, participants were asked to write about things that had had some sort of an impact on them, and it could be smaller or bigger things.[17]

Participants did this exercise every day for a total of 14 days. At the end of the study, the researchers found that those participants who wrote about gratitude boosted their positive emotions. Their happiness and life satisfaction were also enhanced.[17]

This study and many others (especially work by Professor Martin Seligman at the University of Pennsylvania) show that focusing on gratitude can have positive effects in our daily lives. The feeling of gratitude however, can begin to really take over our lives when we experience a traumatic event.

GRATITUDE AND THE RUBBLE AFTER THE EARTHQUAKE

When you experience a difficulty, it can be like an earthquake: all your philosophies and understandings of life can shatter in an instant.[18-19] You start feeling confused about who you are and what your place is in this world. Aspects that are important, such as intimacy, can be disrupted. You might start asking yourself: 'Why did this happen to me?' This can remind us that no matter how much we'd like life to be fair, it's not. The terrible events that befall people (e.g. cheating or bullying, getting into an accident) can destroy our image of a just world. It can destroy people's beliefs.[18-19]

Posttraumatic growth is growth that is spurred on by upsetting or disruptive circumstances, which can harm wellbeing. And we can learn a lot from people who have experienced this kind of growth. I've reflected on the research that's been done in this area, and it seems that people who grow internally tend to take this *active stance* when they're faced with challenges in life. They might feel numb or have lost their bearing and not know which step to take next, but despite this, they try to 'walk through the rubble' after the earthquake: they re-examine their beliefs, they think about what might've caused the difficulty, the meaning of it all and the implications. And while they reflect and try to find a way to integrate the harsh new reality into their lives, they may realize that they're stronger than they thought.[18-19-118] That they can make it through or maybe even discover a new path in life - a key reason for gratitude.

When researchers want to know if people experienced posttraumatic growth, they assess aspects such as the following*[20]:

- New appreciation or gratitude for life: 'I have a greater appreciation for the value of my own life.'
- Changed priorities: e.g. 'I changed my priorities about what is important in life.'
- Greater sense of strength: 'I have a greater feeling of self-reliance.' Or: 'I discovered that I'm stronger than I thought I was.'
- Improved relationships: 'I put more effort into my relationships.'

Appreciation is a core aspect of posttraumatic growth, and can be especially felt after you go through something difficult. People who have suffered trauma may engage in this comparison: how they were before the life-altering event and how they are now. They sometimes use words such as 'selfish', 'sarcastic', 'a jerk' to describe how they had been in the past, before the difficulty.[21] Now, after the fact, they often see themselves as a different person with greater empathy towards others, and a greater understanding for the

* This is based on work by Richard Tedeschi and Lawrence Calhoun: https://onlinelibrary.wiley.com/doi/epdf/10.1002/jts.2490090305

world.[21-119] As you read their stories, a sense of gratitude becomes apparent.

Appreciation often pervades the lives of people who experience challenges. And sometimes the harder the hurdles we go through, the more we can spot opportunities for gratitude. Ellie, a participant with a disability, became more open in one study, and showed an appreciation for becoming a more understanding, kinder individual after the traumatic event. Another participant with paraplegia, Mary, felt grateful that she was able to still take part in adapted sports. Even though she couldn't function as other people could anymore, she was still thankful that she was able to do things on her own.[21]

Comparing yourself to someone else who is worse off than you are now can also make you feel grateful for what you do have in your life. You may also realize that, after the traumatic incident, you've positively transformed in ways you might've never even thought possible. Perhaps you realize that you changed from someone who didn't care about others' feelings to a more considerate and empathetic person.[21]

Appreciation is a key aspect in the context of trauma, and appears to be a real driving force in the lives of people who have faced difficulties. Research on people who experienced traumatic injury showed that the problem didn't hold these people back. Instead, they found opportunities, they formed meaningful bonds with others, they began having a greater appreciation for life. They became truly thankful for the little things in life: for example, seeing colourful butterflies or even hearing themselves breathing.[21] One participant who had experienced trauma beautifully highlighted this aspect:

I have a greater appreciation for life because you realize that it can be taken away or, you know, it can vanish at any point . . . Until you come that close to dying you don't realize what a gift, I mean, just like, not even every day but every breath. Every heartbeat is just a bonus as far as I'm concerned.[21]

Other people in various studies even showed a sense of gratitude for the illness that had befallen them. For example, women in one study talked about how HIV was 'saving their lives' from drug abuse and had put them on a path to recovery.[22] One woman, Carlotta, who had been doing crack cocaine and then found out she had contracted HIV, said:

I decided that after all of the years trying to die, I've got a potential death sentence, but do I really want to die? I thought 'No.' HIV saved my life . . . It clicked that if I wanted to live I had to do something different. I packed up and I moved. I left the drugs alone and haven't taken drugs since. I'm nine years clean . . .[22]

Some of these women used pictures to show what they were going through and how they had changed.[22] In my coaching practice, when we're on the road to self-development and bouncing back from difficulties, I ask people at various points along the way to select a picture. A picture that's representative of the point in life they're at now. For one young man, it was a car on a long, winding road surrounded by trees and gravel, and the sun was shining: he'd travelled a long way and the clouds had cleared up, making way for the sun, but there was still a small stretch of road to get to where he wanted. Using pictures or drawings that you create or engaging in another form of artistic expression, such as dance, can help you understand better what you're experiencing, and help you try to make sense of it all.

Posttraumatic growth can arise in a wide variety of circumstances, and you can grow even in some of the most difficult of times, such as when you're in prison. Diana, a 35-year-old woman who had committed arson in her ex-boyfriend's house (part of her might've done this to seek revenge, because her boyfriend had broken up with her), had been imprisoned and she received therapy in prison. During her time in prison, she began understanding herself better, and listening better to her body.[23] Such positive changes can be a cause for gratitude.

You can feel a sense of thankfulness that you're now able to see what is really important in life. And understand yourself better. And also engage in things that are more meaningful. Take a look at what a study participant with severe injuries said, who showed posttraumatic growth. His injury changed his priorities and he began to focus on more meaningful life aspects, such as close relationships with others:

> Law school is something that I was always going to do. But prior to my injury, it was going to be corporate law [to] see how far I can take this, and I would pull the 80-hour weeks and see how long it would take me to get to $500,000. Now I am totally not into that. I do not want to work in [a large city] even though that is where all the big money jobs are. It is not worth it to me. My priorities have drastically changed . . . My family and my friends and the relationships that I have with my community and giving back. I used to be quite anxious. Stressed all the time about nothing. I always laugh and say that then I broke my back and have real things to worry about.[24-25]

When people go through difficulties in life - whether it's trauma, an illness, or various types of hardships, gratitude and appreciation can make it easier to endure tough times. And it can bring unexpected moments of happiness into what would otherwise be a difficult stretch of time. Gratitude, however, can also play an important role towards the end of our lives.

I find it beautiful to look to older people and see how they handle life, what their words of wisdom are. They have seen and gone through so much, and we can learn a great deal if we lend an ear. The next section is predominantly based on the socio-emotional selectivity theory (theory on how we perceive time and the way that we choose our goals), which Laura Carstensen, Professor of Psychology at Stanford University, and colleagues wrote about.[26] This is combined with my own reflections on gratitude based on discussions and interviews I've had with clients.

GRATITUDE IN OLDER AGE VS. YOUTH AND THE WIDE-OPEN ROAD

Interestingly, as our lives approach the end, gratitude appears to become a key aspect. And the way we perceive our future has a key role to play in this.

As we go through life and the years start racking up, we become increasingly aware of the end. And goals that we might have had when we were younger, such as making new friends or acquiring new knowledge, can start to seem superficial. The goals of adulthood begin to seem less and less important, because they're related to a future which is shrinking. It may not seem relevant anymore how much new knowledge you acquire. Or how many interesting new acquaintances you form connections with, because you might feel like those days of accumulating (whether it's information, material possessions or social connections) are over.

As people become older, their priorities shift: they start to value close bonds with friendships they have already solidified. They choose to pursue activities that have meaning, such as spending time with people who are emotionally close to them. Those activities that don't bring meaning get discarded or are often seen as unimportant.[26]

Older age and living in the present moment

When the end is in sight, we also tend to be more consumed with what's happening in the present moment, as opposed to thinking about the future. We begin to pay greater attention to our emotions. When we get the feeling that time is running out, we start to give greater importance to our feelings and what is going on right now.[26] There are courses and seminars on how to become more present, but sometimes nothing can bring about this awareness of the present moment more than knowing that the end is in sight. As sad as it is to reflect on this, perhaps we need to understand this reality, so that we can jolt ourselves awake and start appreciating what is in front of us now.

Now let's look at perceptions in youth versus older age.

Youth and the wide-open road versus older age

When people are younger, they tend to perceive time and life as a wide-open road in front of them. They set aims that are future-oriented, the future itself is viewed as 'open-ended' and 'expansive'.[26] The possibilities seem endless, you're an explorer setting off on an adventure, making choices and blunders along the way as you're trying to find your footing in this world. It seems exciting. You don't know who or what you will come across. You may develop ambitions for a long future ahead.

However, when you believe the end is near, you tend develop more of a present orientation, as Carstensen et al. write.[26] We become more consumed with the meaningful aspects of life, the emotional side of life. We are 'relieved of concerns about the future'[26] and so begin to prioritize aspects that bring value into our lives and become more preoccupied with how we feel. We are no longer concerned with, as said, accumulating many friends, but rather become focused on those friendships that we already have and nourishing close bonds. In this way, emotional quality rather than quantity takes precedence. As we age, we become less consumed with preparing for a distant future, and instead become preoccupied with being satisfied in the present moment - being thankful for the close bonds that we do have is the essence of gratitude. As Carstensen shows, older people are mostly present-oriented, less concerned than the young with the far distant future.[27] They do not dwell on the past, however, as popular stereotypes suggest. Rather, more than other age groups, they focus on the here and now.[26] Gratitude is often a focus on the here and now, and feeling thankful for what you've got.

This brings things into perspective. Oftentimes, when you're young, you're all about the pursuit of new friends, new ventures and new beginnings, and may strive for this at the expense of your health and other emotional needs. But as life passes us by and we've accumulated various things, and perhaps crossed off various items on our life's to-do list, we see that this isn't really what we've been after all along. It's like a mirage you've been chasing your whole life, and when you get there, the promise of happiness and lifelong satisfaction is still not fulfilled.

As you age, you may give up chasing this 'mirage' and this siren's song of success, rather you just want to be satisfied in the present moment and feel good. This is why in old age, people tend to have goals related to positive feelings, such as appreciation and gratitude. When a distant future is no longer in sight, people begin to prize activities and states that give them a sense of emotional stability.[28] It's interesting that our whole lives we may be consumed with achieving more, and then at the end of our lives, we realize, it's actually not what we may need, after all.

When researchers compared middle-aged and older-aged couples, the latter also showed more positive emotions than the former. Compared to those who were middle-aged, older people had less anger and less disgust, and older couples were more affectionate towards each other even when talking about relationship problems.[26] It's as if, finally, at the end of our lives, we start to realize what is truly of value.

GRATITUDE IN HEALTH AND ILLNESS

Many studies have been written on the subject of gratitude in the context of illness: whether it's gratitude among people suffering from cancer, irritable bowel syndrome or other conditions.

When you're very sick and realize that time is limited, priorities often change, and greater focus on meaningful emotional experiences tends to take precedence. This is why younger people who are ill and perceive the end in sight tend to have similar preferences to older people: they prize those aspects that bring value in their lives, such as close emotional bonds with familiar loved ones. When the future is limited, attention to feeling becomes paramount and emotional aspects of relationships take centre stage.[29] It is plausible to think that such experiences may also evoke a sense of gratitude; a sense of thankfulness that you have people who can fulfil your emotional needs when there's little time left. It is plausible to believe that such experiences may lead to feelings of thankfulness - you're surrounded by family or a close friend who is there to support you.

While you're ill, it can be difficult to divert your mind away from the symptoms or the pain you're experiencing. All you might want is relief, and your mind may be consumed by this. But even in these circumstances, when we take notice of positive moments, such as small positive interactions, this makes room for wellbeing.[30] And it can make room for gratitude. If you're dealing with a chronic illness, when you allow yourself to feel momentarily joyful because of the sun's rays or beautiful flowers outside, it can help. And gratitude is key to this.[30] I came across an article written about people living with multiple sclerosis and psychiatric illnesses; the researchers of the article said: 'It is a matter of attention, of interpretation and of acceptance of the situation in the light of the beauty still found in the middle of a crisis'.[30] When you're going through a tough time, take a moment to look upwards and notice, and enjoy the beauty that this world with its natural wonders often exudes.

Gratitude can also shape your perceptions of the past, and this is important in the context of illness. When you think about the past through a lens of gratitude, even if you're suffering and unwell, memories of love may emerge from the depths of your mind.[30] And these memories may take your mind away from the present difficulties, even if it's just for a brief moment.

Gratitude can shape your perceptions of the past.

Conclusion

Having feelings of gratitude or appreciation may make it easier to bear life's burdens. It can remind people of the little joys in life, the moments we may take for granted. Gratitude can help people tackle adversity and has been linked to positive emotions and happiness.[31]

When people are faced with hardship, having a grateful disposition can help. It can help us keep going even when it may be difficult to do so. It lays the foundation for a more positive road forward.

The next chapter will focus on strategies for bringing gratitude into your life.

CHAPTER 3

GRATITUDE: STRATEGIES

This chapter will present strategies for gratitude. It will help you develop a sense of thankfulness and tap into the power of awe.

EMERGENCY STRATEGIES

A simple and fast way to bring gratitude into your life is to use these in-the-moment strategies.

- Write a gratitude letter to someone who helped you in the past or who you feel appreciative for. In a study done by Martin Seligman, professor at Pennsylvania University, he showed that people who had written a gratitude letter to someone they had 'never properly thanked',[32] and then delivered the letter to the recipient, were happier and showed fewer depressive symptoms one week and one month after they did this.
- Carry out an act of kindness. For example, this could be giving a homeless person something to eat or bringing seeds to feed the birds.

COPING INSTINCTIVELY VS. INTENTIONALLY

To deal with stress, problems or challenges in life, we cope. We have *instinctive coping* strategies that we engage in on autopilot, or that have been programmed into us as children: maybe we saw our parents handling or coping with situations in particular ways, and we emulated them.

For example, the father of a woman I coach coped with stressful or somewhat difficult situations by avoiding them. If his life wasn't going well, he wouldn't make time for gratitude or practise other helpful coping strategies, because he thought it wouldn't make a difference (instead, he would chronically block out the issues). Karla learned to do the same.

Many of us react without thinking twice, we behave on autopilot or repeat things we've seen others do while we were growing up. Instinctive coping is what comes naturally to us. But we can override this; *we can choose to cope intentionally*. We can choose to do things on purpose because we know they are good for our wellbeing. In this way, knowledge is power. We can switch from the instinctive coping that we do on autopilot to intentional coping.

It's about actively changing our thinking patterns, our emotional responses to setbacks, and our ways of coping that don't serve us well. Even though we've got learned coping tendencies, in that space when we're deciding how to respond to a problem, we can instead choose to veer off course and try a different strategy. Intentional coping is what allows us to grow.

LONG-TERM STRATEGIES

Use these strategies to bring more gratitude into your life. Take the time to jot down any reflections or thoughts that arise as you go through them.

#1 Focus on what you have instead of what you're lacking

Instead of thinking about what you lack, focus on what you do have. For example, if you're not in perfect health, are there areas of your health that *do* make you feel grateful?

What are other aspects you could feel a sense of appreciation for? You might not have a partner right now, but perhaps you have an understanding friend. Let's do a gratitude exercise. I invite you now to make a list of five things that you are feeling grateful for in this moment - it doesn't matter how big or small. Then focus on each one in turn, and write a list of the feelings and thoughts you get as you reflect on each thing.

Steps towards gratitude	
What are you grateful for that you have in your life now? It could be a moment of joy with your pet, a sunny day, a delicious cake, etc.	What feelings and thoughts arise in you as you reflect on this?
1.	
2.	
3.	
4.	
5.	

#2 Bring awe into your life

A manifestation of appreciation is awe.[33] It can be helpful to cultivate feelings of awe if you're going through a tough time. So what is awe? It can be a feeling of transcendence, a sense of elation, a sense that life is worth living. And that sometimes, life can amaze us in unexpected ways. Noticing those moments is part of learning to be more appreciative, and this can have a positive impact on our mood and wellbeing.

For example, you may be out for a hike and feel a deep sense of connection with nature. Maybe you've reached the peak of the hiking trail and are looking out over a mass of trees beneath you, and all of a sudden, you are overtaken by unexpected emotions. You are overtaken by a state of awe. The beauty of the nature is developing this highly appreciative or grateful feeling within you.

Another way to tap into this feeling of awe is by listening to a beautiful piece of music or seeing a piece of art that moves you. Suddenly, you may realize you're feeling a deep sense of gratitude for the exceptional talent of the artist who created this. You may get a feeling of transcendence: you're moving beyond the here and now, you feel like you are transported to a new level.

The feeling of awe comes about when you're astounded or moved by something, such as by nature or a beautiful piece of music.

Experiencing awe can have positive health effects. It can lead to lower levels of proinflammatory cytokines,[34] which are generated by immune system cells in our bodies.[35] Proinflammatory cytokines can make illnesses worse,[36] therefore it is beneficial when we can combat these. Tapping into awe and bringing more of this into your life can be one way to help tackle those harmful bodily entities.

Experiences that elicit a sense of awe can capture your attention and make you feel as if you're completely immersed in the situation – and this has an impact on your brain and **sense of self**.[37] Say you're next to an ocean, staring off into the distance at the roaring waves. You start to get goosebumps and begin to forget about yourself. Or perhaps you're standing on the edge of a tall cliff and peer down at the vastness below – suddenly, you start to feel small.[37] This is *'the small self'* effect.[38] When we get feelings of awe, these not only appear to alter our perceptions of ourselves, but also have an influence on our brain at a neural level.[37] Feelings of awe have been found to lower the activity in the default mode network, which is a brain network believed to be linked to our sense of self.[39]

Therefore, tapping into awe can have various effects on our senses and awareness, as well as bodies. So try and bring more of these awe experiences into your life. Can you go to a concert? Make time in your weekend to get outside in nature? Perhaps go and visit a gallery?

What other instances can you think of that can produce such feelings? What else can you do to bring awe into your life? Why not write a few down here.

Weekend (Indicate the date below)	Activities to bring awe into my life	Accountability (Place a checkmark if you did the activity)
1.	1.	
2.	2.	

Weekend (Indicate the date below)	Activities to bring awe into my life	Accountability (Place a checkmark if you did the activity)
3.	3.	
4.	4.	
5.	5.	

#3 Go outside with a young child

This strategy presents another way for bringing awe – and therefore, gratitude – into your life. Children are amazed by many aspects of this world. Everything is new to them and simple things, such as a bee that has just landed on the dewy grass in the morning, or a small bird that is peeking out through the tree branches or a shiny conker, can make them go into a state of awe. If you spend time with a small child, you might catch some of the awe-inspiring feelings as well. So go outside with a young child and watch this small being be inspired and fascinated by the world; let your guard down and join in. Notice what the child is noticing. This helps to take you away for a while from adult responsibilities and burdens, and opens your eyes up to the earth we inhabit, and that we often take for granted. It opens you up to gratitude. Is there a family member or friend that you could do this with? Or your own child, of course – can you make time to get outside this weekend?

#4 Create thoughts of gratitude before bedtime

Gratitude has been linked to better sleep; you sleep for longer and you get better quality sleep.[40-41] You also tend to have more energy throughout the day.[41] If you're grateful, your mind searches for more pleasant aspects and thoughts before bedtime, and this can make you sleepy.

One way to practise gratitude is to think of three things that happened each day that you are grateful for, every night before going to bed. This can change your thought processes from negative to more positive, and can help your brain switch to a calmer mode, ready for restful sleep. Gratitude has also been linked to the release of dopamine and serotonin, which play a role in your sleep-wake cycle. So tonight, when you lie down in bed, think of three things that you were grateful for today. It could be that your home is quiet, you had an enjoyable dinner, you chatted with a pleasant neighbour. Anything you like, big or small.

#5 Use comparisons to tap into gratitude

When people go through a tough time - whether it's a difficult split, abuse or other hardships - it can be helpful to meet people who are further along in the recovery process than you, as it can give you a feeling of thankfulness and hope that it is possible to bounce back from your difficulty. By the same token, when you meet people who are further behind, this can instill a sense of **gratitude about how far you've come**. And how can you meet these people? Through a support group, which enables you to talk to others about their and your experience.

Sheryle Vilenica at the Queensland University of Technology studied people who experienced childhood sexual abuse, and suggested that when people are part of therapeutic support groups, they may examine their progress in their healing journey by looking to other people who are further along or earlier on in the recovery process.[42] This can serve as a check-in point. Therefore, celebrating small wins and taking time for gratitude can encourage us to keep going.

#6 Want to become happier? Engage in experiences that make you feel grateful.

Let's start accumulating experiences of gratitude now. Let's start building up a memory bank of cherished experiences to look back on with gratitude, should we need to draw on this resource when we're going through (other) tough times in the future.

Gratitude is directly linked to happiness.[31] But this aspect is in stark contrast to what we often believe: that it is accumulating material possessions, *not* experiences, that makes us feel grateful and happy.

If possessions made us happy, we would expect to see our level of happiness go up in direct proportion to the number of items or material possessions we own. Or we might think that the greater our bank account balance, the more satisfied and grateful we'd feel – grateful for the comfort and luxury that money can buy. Ryan Howell, Professor of Psychology at San Francisco State University, says: 'People still believe that more money will make them happy, even though 35 years of research has suggested the opposite.'[43]

It turns out that it isn't necessarily the number of items or the amount of money that makes you happy. Rather, it's how you spend it – whether you use it to immerse yourself in experiences that can make you feel alive and, I would add, grateful; in other words, life experiences. Research shows that when we buy life experiences rather than material possessions,[43] we're often happier. So it isn't the number of shirts or cars that you buy and own that are linked to your happiness level. Rather, it's taking part in life experiences that you can look back on and cherish.[43] Experiences that evoke a sense of gratitude.

For example, life experiences such as the snorkelling lessons you took that allowed you to observe underwater life or the orchard you visited while you went sightseeing in a neighbouring city. These can stay with you for a longer period, and you can look back on them with feelings of appreciation and delight.[44]

Conclusion

Gratitude has been written about by so many, and we often hear that we need to feel grateful because it's good for our wellbeing. This is, no doubt, positive advice. But oftentimes we're not really told *why* we need to feel grateful, how it can change our lives in the context of trauma, and make us feel happier in our day-to-day. Knowing about the science of gratitude can help us live more fulfilled, peaceful lives. And practising strategies for gratitude - such as tapping into this feeling of awe or transcendence, one of the most profound feelings on earth - can give us a sense of aliveness.

CHAPTER 4

RELATIONSHIPS: THE SCIENCE BEHIND THIS

We've taken a look at the first stage of **G**ROW (Gratitude), and now it's time to turn our attention to **R**elationships.

Relationships are an important part of our lives. From infanthood, relationships shape us and we in turn, shape the relationships we're in. Relationships are composed of multiple key aspects. In this chapter, we are going to look at our human need for connection and how trauma can get in the way of relationships. We will also look at: the factors that make us want to take revenge on someone and the effects revenge can have on people; venting when you're frustrated or angry; and our online relationships.

Our human need for connection

Relationships are important to human beings. Relationships with other people can make us feel secure and give us a feeling of belonging. On the next page is an illustration of Maslow's famous hierarchy of needs,[120] which shows the needs that human beings have.

In this illustration, we see that, at the bottom of the pyramid, we all have physiological needs (we all have a basic need for food, air, water, shelter, etc.). As we go up the pyramid, we see that we have needs for safety, such as feeling secure and in control of our lives. When these are satisfied, we then focus on meeting needs for love and belonging. We want to feel like we're connected to people. So we might seek social connection through intimate, warm relationships, friendships or groups.[45]

As human beings, we have a desire to belong and be part of a group or community – it could be a community of ten people or a community of two.

Being part of social networks can have a significant influence on us. Social support can enhance our *resilience to stress*.[46] When we feel supported, this can help us cope when we're going through tough times. We start seeing the difficult or stressful situation in a different light – a more positive light.[47-48]

Researchers at Harvard University have shown that having strong, supportive bonds is also associated with a good life. George Vaillant, Professor of Psychiatry at Harvard Medical School says that, 'Warm, intimate relationships are the most important prologue to a good life.'[49] In 1972, George Vaillant became the director of one of the longest-running studies on adult development, the Harvard Grant Study. The study started in 1938 and its initial aim was to find the recipe to a 'happy and healthy life'.[50-51] Over 200 Harvard students, the study's participants, were followed over the course of their lives. They had their medical records examined, they filled out questionnaires and gave interviews. And through this process we learned about these people's ups and downs, and the things that made life worth living – importantly, relationships was one of them.[50-51]

This research showed that warm relationships, among other factors, are key in determining later success – in particular, economic success. It appears that experiencing warm relationships and strong bonds aren't just good for our mental health. Having good family relationships when you grow up also appears to be linked to making more money later on. In this study, the men who had good relationships with their siblings and mothers tended to have higher incomes than those with poor relationships. So having positive relationships isn't just good for our wellbeing; it seems to have a spill-over effect and touch seemingly unrelated areas of our lives.[50]

We've seen that if we don't have supportive relationships, this may have an undesirable impact on our economic success. However, not having friends is linked to another major aspect: loneliness. Research suggests that feeling disconnected is as harmful to health as smoking up to 15 cigarettes per day.[52] Despite the negative health impacts, many people are lonely across the globe. According to the World Health Organization, 1 in 3 older people experience loneliness.[53] Also, about 9-14% of adolescents in various parts of the world (for example, countries in the Americas, Africa, Eastern Mediterranean, Europe, South-East Asia, Western Pacific) are lonely.[54] And loneliness can stem from a number of causes, including experiencing something traumatic.

Trauma, isolation and other consequences
When something traumatic happens in people's lives, their relationships can become affected. In a study by researchers from Ryerson University and Harvard Medical school, the real story of Lauren and her husband Bradley is described.[55] This couple experienced trauma, and isolation became a central aspect of Lauren's life. 'Relationship' played a key role in their story. Here's what happened, as outlined by the study's authors, Amy Brown-Bowers, Steffany Fredman, Sonya Wanklyn and Candice Monson, in the *Journal of Clinical Psychology*[55]:

Lauren and Bradley eagerly awaited the birth of their son. But when Lauren experienced abdominal cramping one day and went to the hospital to get checked, everything started going downhill

Self-actualization
desire to become the most that one can be

Esteem
respect, self-esteem, status, recognition, strength, freedom

Love and belonging
friendship, intimacy, family, sense of connection

Safety needs
personal security, employment, resources, health, property

Physiological needs
air, water, food, shelter, sleep, clothing, reproduction

Source: Plateresca / Getty Images / ThoughtCo.
https://www.thoughtco.com/maslows-hierarchy-of-needs-4582571.

from there. The staff couldn't detect a fetal heartbeat and shortly thereafter, they induced labour in her. The fear, horror and shock that she experienced as a result of these events had a profound effect on her.[55]

In the aftermath of the stillbirth, Lauren swung between feeling very angry to feeling sad or irritated. She experienced a range of emotions and began isolating herself from others. She felt that those closest to her had betrayed her, and her relationship with Bradley started to fall apart. Lauren didn't feel understood by her husband and this caused her to move away from him – she felt alone.[55]

The stillbirth not only shook her beliefs in a just world, but she started questioning whether it was her fault that this had happened. She felt betrayed by God, and she didn't feel understood by her husband who coped with the stillbirth differently (in contrast to her, he turned to close others for support). So her relationship with God and her husband took a downward turn.[55]

Her husband felt that it was his duty to see his wife happy again, and whenever she'd bring up negative thoughts or feelings, he'd try to find ways to 'fix it'. He tried to find solutions to her problems. But this approach only made Lauren feel angry and frustrated – she wanted to simply be heard, not given advice. So she started distancing herself from him. And she began avoiding telling him what was on her mind.[55]

Bradley's desire to problem-solve stemmed out of wanting to be a good husband. He felt that if he couldn't fix Lauren's troubles, he himself had failed as a husband.[55] And this brings to mind my mother's experience with cancer. When she sometimes recounts to her friends about the pain or breathlessness she's experiencing, they tell her to just 'be more optimistic' or 'try treatment A, B or C'. Her friends are trying to be helpful, but all this does is make her feel like she's not really understood. It makes her feel *alone*. When my mother tells me about these experiences, she says that, 'People just want to feel understood and heard. They don't want to be given advice', especially if it's unasked.

The other thing is, sometimes people want to talk about difficult trauma-related feelings they're experiencing, but we may think that if we join them in this, it hinders their recovery. So we don't engage, because we want to get them out of this loop of negative thinking. But only focusing on the positive (trying to 'cheerlead') and ignoring the negative can stand in the way of the healing journey. In Lauren and Bradley's case, this is exactly what happened. When Bradley avoided talking about negative feelings with Lauren (including his own anxiety that he was experiencing as a result of the traumatic event), this made Lauren feel alone. It eroded their emotional closeness.[55]

Lauren had post-traumatic stress disorder. She experienced flashbacks and nightmares, and she started avoiding things that reminded her of the traumatic event: anything pregnancy-related and even individuals who appeared to be content with their lives. She found it hard to see happy people when her own life was going so badly.[55] This may have contributed to feelings of loneliness in her.

Lauren and Bradley started working with a therapist, and began rebuilding their relationship. Bradley learned to listen better whenever Lauren wanted to unburden. Together, they also began facing their fears. Instead of avoiding uncomfortable situations (e.g. the places that reminded Lauren of the trauma), they began to slowly expose themselves to these. For example, one day they drove up to the parking lot of the hospital where the stillbirth had taken place.[55] When we're dealing with such difficulties, it's often easier to face them with a supportive individual by our side, such as Bradley – and this is where relationships come in handy.

With her husband by her side, Lauren was also taught to let go of the need for control and certainty in her life. The stillbirth appeared to have made her cautious of hoping (and taking positive steps forward) in case everything took a downward turn again. So when she found out that she was pregnant a second time, she didn't want to take the necessary vitamins and go for a timely ultrasound at first, because what if the pregnancy didn't work out again? It was a defence mechanism – it seemed she was protecting herself from getting too hopeful and happy in case the ending was a bad one.[51] Maybe superstition had a role to play too, I reflected while reading the article. Sometimes we might tell ourselves, 'If I do X or Y, then things will work out better.'

In therapy, Lauren was taught to approach unhelpful ideas or thoughts with an air of curiosity – to poke and prod at them from all angles to see if they had any merit.[55] With Bradley by her side, she reflected on the fact that some people who don't take proper care of themselves - who abuse substances and drink - have healthy babies, while others who have lots of money and access to the best medical care can have miscarriages. Working through these thoughts together, no doubt, helped to strengthen their relationship.[55]

Lauren and Bradley challenged unhelpful thoughts together; she reflected that, sometimes, no matter how much effort we put into something or however much money someone has, the outcome can still turn out undesirable.[55] All we can do is take the necessary steps in the right direction, and then **let the chips fall where they may**.

Reflecting on this made Lauren realize that she could let go of trying to control outcomes. Lauren realized that she did, in fact, care about her second pregnancy and that she did want to take the necessary steps to ensure it would be a good pregnancy.[55] So her relationship with herself also improved. She started doing what was right for her health and the unborn baby. Lauren started taking the necessary vitamins for the pregnancy.[55]

The ending to this story was a happy one. Lauren gave birth to a baby girl, and she and her husband were overjoyed by this. With help, they learned how to bounce back and get their relationship back on track.[55]

We can gather from this story how important having someone by our side is when we're going through something difficult. It helps to talk through things with a close other. However, trauma can also disrupt our relationships, and working with a third party such as a professional can help get our connections with people back on track.

REVENGE

We've looked at the positive when it comes to relationships, so now let's switch our attention to the other side of the coin: the downside. Let's turn to a topic that can play a key role in the context of trauma and is very much part of relationships: revenge.

People ask me about this quite often - others have wronged them and they're thinking of getting their own back in some way. But is it ever a good idea to do so? In the context of our relationship with other people, when should we fight back, say our piece or get revenge?

If someone has upset you or caused you trauma, it may be tempting to do so. If you've had a difficult upbringing, or you've been bullied by friends or co-workers, and these experiences traumatized you, should you pay the wrongdoer back?

If you feel like someone took away your opportunities in life, or damaged your relationships or damaged *you* in some way, fantasies of revenge may take over. But as we'll see later in the chapter, getting back at someone who hurt us might theoretically *seem* like it's a good idea - in reality, it's not. Causing suffering to an individual who betrayed or harmed us can feel momentarily rewarding - we're getting some sort of justice - but these feelings are transitory. The pleasure dissipates quickly. And we're back where we started: with the low mood and, on top of that, we see that the plan for vengeance was in vain. **We could still be dealing with the consequences of the trauma, and so getting back at the offender *doesn't erase the tragic reality of* what's happened**.[56-114]

Revenge can show up in a number of ways. Maybe someone close to us passed away and we're blaming another individual for this. Some people see revenge as a way of showing unwavering allegiance to the person who has passed, a fierce loyalty to the relationship that is no more. They may believe that, by harming the wrongdoer, they are carrying out the wishes and bringing justice to the loved one who has died. But this can be borne out of a difficulty to accept that the cherished friend or family member has really passed away. We're still acting on the loved one's behalf, as if this person were alive and telling us what to do. As if we're helping the deceased get closure.[56-115] But this is an impossible thing because this individual is no longer here.

As humans, we want to live in a safe world, and often assume life is fair and predictable. We want to believe that our loved ones die because of natural causes or old age, not because of another individual's actions or mistakes. This assumption of predictability enables us to feel in control. If we don't feel this security and orderliness in life, we can start to feel distressed.[57]

When someone inflicts pain on a loved one or harms *us*, and we become traumatized by this, this can shake our worldview and our belief system. A traumatic event can make it difficult to still think life is fair, or that if you do good deeds, life will reward you. When a traumatic event turns our world upside down, then revenge can be a way of hanging onto that belief of life being fair. If someone does something bad, we want this person to get payback. And so, by enacting revenge we can still cling onto our old beliefs of fairness.[56-57]

We assume life is fair, but it's not.
Letting go of such assumptions can
make it easier to let go of revenge fantasies.
And move on with life.

A study looked at participants who were assessed before the 9/11 terrorist attacks; the researchers examined how strongly the participants believed in a just world. Having a belief in a just world refers to this faith that the world is stable and orderly, and that people get what they deserve. The participants in this study were assessed on items[57] that measured things, such as[62]:

- 'I feel the world treats people fairly'
- 'I feel that people get what they deserve'
- 'I feel that when people meet with misfortune, they have brought it upon themselves'

These participants were assessed using various instruments before the attacks and again, shortly afterwards. The findings showed that those participants who had the strongest beliefs in a just world also suffered more after the attacks: they showed the highest distress and had the strongest desire for revenge. Why can this be? A reason is that when life deals you a blow and especially a blow to any strong beliefs you may have, you can be left without secure footing in this world. And so to bring back justice and a sense of stability, you desire revenge.[57]

However, as much as traumatic events can anger us and we desire revenge, the perpetrators can still remain unscathed and without punishment – as can happen in cases of child abuse. Kids who have been abused quickly learn that life isn't fair, and that they're on their own; there's no one that can watch their backs and protect them from danger. Powerlessness and shame can play a central role in the narratives of people who have been hurt or betrayed by others.[56-114]

So a reason why people might want to seek revenge is to redress some of the hurt and shame they've been subjected to and get closure. They may feel they have unfinished business and believe that through vengeance, they heal.

People can sometimes seek revenge to get closure. They may have unfinished business and believe that by getting their own back in some way, they will feel better. But the opposite happens.

Revenge is 'a dish best served cold' is an expression that you might be familiar with. The French diplomat Charles Maurice de Talleyrand-Périgord, who was born in the 18th century, used to say it. But does revenge really make us feel better?

People who fantasize about revenge may think that it will make them feel better after they've engaged in it. But actually, the opposite is true. People can be poor forecasters of their emotions and are prone to misprediction. Even though we might think we'll feel a sense of pleasure after carrying out an act of vengeance – and we might indeed feel some momentary pleasure while carrying out the vengeful act, as we've seen – this tends to be very short-lived. People who think about how they will get their revenge on someone, and then carry out their plan, make it more difficult for themselves to *mentally disengage from the incident*.[58] You might indeed feel better in the moment as you're getting even, but actually after a bit of time, you end up feeling worse. After you've exacted your revenge, you might not be able to stop thinking about what's happened. Ruminations can start taking over and this may darken your mood even more.

It seems that revenge comes back to haunt people like a boomerang. However, if you don't retaliate, it's easier to move on. Your mind gets freed up from focusing on the person who has wronged you. If your mind moves on to something else, this can distract you from the anger you're feeling towards your offender. And in this way, your negative emotions can lose some of their potency.[58-59]

Does venting help?

Revenge can be seen as a way of releasing pent-up frustration or letting off steam. It's been theorized that when something frustrates or angers us, we build up pressure within us. And in order to liberate ourselves from the pressure, we need to let it out somehow – otherwise, we could explode from the anger. This is why, many years ago, you might've heard advice that people should take their anger out on an object or vent – so instead of hitting an individual, you'd be encouraged to hit a punching bag or scream in your room. This, it's been believed, contributes to catharsis. And the cathartic release of feelings would allow you to let go of this built-up inner toxicity. If you had pent-up anger (as people often do when they're feeling vengeful), releasing these feelings would help you feel better – or so it was thought.[59] Advice such as this is sometimes still given today.

Sigmund Freud, the famous psychoanalyst, thought that releasing hostile feelings was better than letting them build inside you. But what later research discovered was that this cathartic release and blowing off steam actually wasn't so cathartic – it could make things worse.[59] So instead of feeling calmer after indulging your aggression (for example, by hitting your mattress and imagining your wrongdoer is receiving those blows), you could actually end up feeling more aggressive.[59]

VENTING YOUR ANGER CAN BE COUNTERPRODUCTIVE

This phenomenon has been studied by Dr Brad Bushman at Iowa State University. He's done extensive research on human aggression and violence, and has been part of a US presidential committee on gun violence.[60] In a study done by him, 600 people were asked to write an essay and, after they finished the essay, they were led to believe that it would be given to someone else to evaluate. When the researchers came back with the evaluations, the ratings were negative; all essays had received poor evaluations. There was even a comment included on the assignments that said: 'This is one of the worst essays I have read!'[59] This was done to trigger feelings of anger in the participants who had written the pieces.

Then the participants who wrote the essays were divided into three groups. Each person in the first group was shown the picture of an individual and were told that this person was the one who had criticized the essay. The people in this first group were then instructed to hit a punching bag while thinking about the individual who they thought had evaluated their work. A second group was also instructed to hit a punching bag, but this time were told to hit the bag and think about becoming physically fit - and were shown a picture of an individual engaging in physical activity. The third group didn't do anything - they just sat quietly for a couple of minutes with the experimenter. Then after this, everyone (individually) took part in a competitive game with the person who they were led to believe had criticised their essay. And during the game, participants were allowed to blast loud noises aimed at the other person. It turns out that the people who were told to hit the punching bag and think about the wrongdoer's face were the angriest and also experienced aggression. Venting by hitting a punching bag and thinking about the offender did not, in fact, boost their mood. Interestingly, the people who just sat quietly instead of retaliating or doing anything about their moods fared the best. They had the lowest levels of anger and aggression. So it seems that venting by punching an inanimate object and imagining an enemy's face on it is not so good for the mind, after all. It can actually make things worse and lead to a nosedive in how you're feeling.[59]

Instead of venting, it's better to shift the spotlight from the offender back onto yourself.

Instead of venting, think about how you can get closer to your own goals and dreams, and let go of everything else. This also holds true if you're thinking about seeking revenge. After all, the saying that **the best revenge is living well** couldn't ring truer.

Online relationships

Let's switch gears now. I am going to close this chapter with a final key aspect: our online world. This is an important topic, because many people tend to live their lives online. And the online world can be a source of traumatic bullying or harassment for some people. On top of that, social media addiction is a real problem. Therefore, looking at our relationships in the context of the online world is important and needs to be discussed. Research that examined studies from 32 nations showed that percentage estimates for social media addiction vary widely and even reach 31%.[61] Certain online social media platforms have really taken off and are extremely popular with the young crowd. In the UK, Instagram, TikTok and YouTube tend to be the go-to places for news among teens aged 12-15.[62] In the US, a survey of over 1000 teens aged 13-17 that took place in April-May 2022, found that 95% of teens use YouTube. Many teens also use TikTok and 16% of them are on it 'almost constantly'.[63] People around the world regularly engage with social media, and while some of its impact is highly beneficial (for example, keeping people connected, learning new things), it can also have downsides (it can lead to negative emotions, such as sadness and guilt).[64]

This online world can have an impact on how you see yourself and also the bonds you have with other people.

I would like to share with you messages I received from people over the years related to this. First, here is a message I received from Leon about how social media can be like an alcoholic fix:

I realized I have this habit: every time something negative in my life happens and I get depressed or down, I go to a messaging app for a fix. Usually, this sends me into an even worse emotional spiral because no one writes to me (or at least not the person I'm expecting a message from). Now that I realized this about myself, whenever I'm sad I know I'll get the urge to check all these messaging apps. And when this happens, I resist the initial impulse to do so and then the feeling passes. I feel proud and I feel stronger every time I overcome the urge.

Social media can feel like a fix. If you're feeling lonely or isolated, or something goes badly in an aspect of your life, you may be tempted to rush to one of these platforms for instant gratification. But then seeing other people's posts of their supposedly perfect lives may get you even more down.

We've heard that social media can have benefits – such as making you feel supported and giving you opportunities to share with others what you're going through.[65] But there are also downsides.

One of the downsides is the comparison effect: we see others' posts and may feel our own lives are lacking by comparison. But it is worth remembering that these posts are often highlight reels of other people's lives, they don't represent the full reality. The posts can make it seem as if everyone is happy and successful, and this in turn, can make you feel inferior and dissatisfied about your own life and even your own body. The use of a popular social media platform that is used by more than a billion people around the world has been linked to issues with body image, especially in teenage girls.[66] When we're comparing our own bodies to carefully selected and airbrushed images of people online, this can be harmful.[66]

The term 'Facebook envy'[67] has also been coined to show how social media can impact us and our relationships with others. When people go on social networking sites and see images of friends' perfect jobs, perfect partners, perfect anything, this may not feel so good - especially if your life isn't going as well. The browsing can fuel painful feelings of envy, hence the term, Facebook envy.[68] But this phenomenon isn't specific to Facebook; we can deduce that these feelings may be triggered by any platform that encourages this comparison effect with other people.

The comparison effect may be especially harmful for those with poor mental health.[68] If you have depression, then the online world can be a risky place. If you're suffering, your surrounding environment should be one of peace and calm. When you're online, the environment can feel irritating: people are showing off and this may increase the risk of experiencing feelings of envy.

There could be a number of reasons behind these effects: when we're comparing our own lives to other people's rosy, online lives, our own shortcomings begin to stand out. Social media platforms can also create a sense of ranking among people - this is because of features such as follower counts and the number of likes you get on posts. If you have only a few people listed as your 'friends' or your posts are not receiving likes, this may make you feel embarrassed and unhappy. There may be this feeling of an imaginary ladder that's being created, placing some people above others depending on their online popularity.

Getting a 'like' on these platforms can also feel good: you're getting a shot of dopamine, a brain chemical linked to pleasure. We enjoy getting those pleasurable, good feelings when someone likes something we posted, and the more we experience these good feelings, the more we may crave them, and seek them. A study that took place at the University of California, Los Angeles's' Ahmanson-Lovelace Brain Mapping Centre examined 32 teenagers aged 13-18. The researchers looked at their brain activity using fMRIs while the teens were engaging with social media. Teens who saw that their own photos were getting lots of likes showed activity in many parts of the brain, including an area linked to reward.[69-70] Other research has also shown that being constantly online and engaging heavily with social media platforms can have an impact on the brain.

Fear of missing out

The other problem with social media is that it can be linked to a fear of missing out a.k.a. FOMO.[71] You might choose not to be online. But at the same time, if you're not online and there are events pages that you're not seeing, then you're not able to sign up and participate with your friends; you might worry that you're not able to make new friendships.

During my undergraduate degree, I started regularly using a social networking site. I would receive notifications to events going on, and because I couldn't always go to these, I started feeling that maybe I was missing out. As I grew older, I decided at times to take complete breaks from social media. And during those times, it didn't feel at all that I was missing out – in fact, it was the opposite. I felt a sense of calmness and my mind was at peace. I still use social media sometimes, but I go on it less frequently than before.

Social media networking sites may also be addictive, and this is another aspect that is worth considering. I would like to share with you messages I received from people relating to this. Here is Sophie:

> I remember that every time I saw that bright red circle showing the number of messages I'd received, it would make me go crazy; it would make me feel a craving for something which was almost painful. I couldn't wait to open the message and see WHAT it had in it and WHO it was from. More often than not, I'd be disappointed, not having received messages from the people I wanted to hear. But when I got a message from Neal, suddenly my adrenaline would rush to the top of my head, a surge of happiness would shoot through me, my sleepiness would turn into alertness. I would float while the world around me didn't exist or seem to matter anymore. That got me hooked to Facebook's messaging system. I was living and dying for that bright red circle showing the number of messages I received.
>
> That's why the habit that I found by far the hardest to break was Facebook addiction. I also realized that it was an illusion that I was popular and getting invited to all these events (they were just mass invitations). I never ended up going to most of them, and none of the people I interacted with on Facebook were close to me. I'd see my actual friends face to face.
>
> When I decided to stop messaging through Facebook (I used to do that a lot with my friend Rebecca), something happened. I realized that Rebecca and I were never seeing each other

anymore. When we stopped communicating over Facebook, I realized that we had sort of drifted apart and I felt empty. I actually got a little mad at her, thinking that she'd abandoned me. But after deciding to let go of Facebook, I ended up thinking a lot less about Rebecca in the two months after I'd made that decision. I no longer felt neglected by her or other people on Facebook who seemed to lead their own lives (happy lives as you could see from their pictures in which they looked busy and successful and showing off their boyfriends or girlfriends). I had slowly forgotten or thought less about these 'electronic' people and began leading my own life.

Now that I've finally let go of Facebook, I feel happier. Now that I finally let go of it, I feel happier. Only when Rebecca called me today, did I start thinking about her again. And I was happy when she called, not because she was throwing me a bone and paying some attention to me. But because I was busy living my own life and living in reality instead of some imaginary, electronic world.

Here's Mara:

I told myself that I wouldn't check Facebook until 6pm Thursday, but I don't know what's wrong with my willpower. I couldn't wait until Thursday and checked it last night. I couldn't help myself – like an addict, I rushed to the log-in screen of Facebook and my fingers were running over the keyboard as I swiftly put in my username and password. Then I checked it again all day today under the pretence that I needed to get back to my friends about a party on Saturday. Breaking my own word makes it hard to trust myself. And social media makes it hard for me to keep my own word.

So how can we use social media in a way that is helpful for us? And particularly, in a way that is helpful for our relationships?

Using social media to maintain or strengthen connections is beneficial. If you're feeling supported online and your interactions are positive, this is of course a good sign. The key thing to ask yourself is, though: are you spending *too much* time online and not enough in the real world? Are you making enough time to meet and speak with people face to face?[65] Balance is key.

By becoming aware of our patterns, we can choose a different course of action.

The online world can make us feel dissatisfied with own lives. However, it can also be a source of excitement and connection - a place where people across the world come together and interact. Social media platforms have really taken off, and more and more people spend time on them. When we use them wisely, they can be great sources of connection and networking.

Conclusion

Relationships can provide a buffer against high stress, and they help us navigate challenging periods.

Being part of social networks is important for our mental health and gives us a sense of community. Relationships give us a sense of belonging and can make us feel safe. When we focus on building strong connections with people who treat us well, this is essential for our wellbeing and it is essential for our health. The next chapter will present strategies on developing a good relationship with yourself and others.

CHAPTER 5

RELATIONSHIPS: STRATEGIES

This chapter looks at strategies for creating and strengthening our relationships with other people. We will look at how we can sow the seeds for new relationships, forge new connections, and why it is important to have mercy towards ourselves and how this translates into better relationships with other people. As relationships are a central theme in trauma, I am providing strategies in this chapter to help you move forward and strengthen bonds with others. And to learn what to do if there's no one around to lean on in the midst of difficulties.

EMERGENCY STRATEGIES

Relationships are a complex topic, but if you need strategies to move forward in this area, here are two exercises. Even though they may seem simple, they lead to profound changes in our connections with others.

- **Accept your and other people's feelings**. Our relationships with other people start with the relationship we have with ourselves. This is one of the most important things to remember in the context of forming and developing strong bonds with others. When you start to accept yourself - in particular, when you start to accept the true feelings arising in you, this is when you also begin to accept the feelings arising in other people. When you start to take the feelings you've got, whether anger or sadness, and gently hold these feelings in your hands like an empathetic parent picking up a crying baby, you start to be more able to tolerate other people's emotions too. If you can stop seeing the emotions arising in you in a negative light, this is also when you can begin to accept the inner world of others.

- If someone close to you has been through trauma and this person would like to unburden to you, **practise simply listening without giving advice**. In the previous chapter, we met Lauren and her husband Bradley. They started working with a therapist, and learned strategies that allowed them to better understand the trauma and how to move past it. They were taught how to communicate better with one another: Bradley learned to *just listen without giving advice*.

LONG-TERM STRATEGIES

Let's look at long-term strategies for creating and strengthening relationships. If you're going through trauma, how can you use relationships in a way that provides you with support? Which people should you keep close to you as you move through life?

#1 Talk about it

When we're going through tough times, turning to relationships can help us bounce back more easily. Talking about what you went through with someone you trust, such as a close friend or family member, can not only deepen your bond, but it can help you get a better perspective on the problem you're facing.

If the trauma has caused you to distance yourself from your partner or other people in your life, then turning to a support group can be a good option. Sometimes people in support groups find it helpful to talk about the event itself, while other times, they wish to focus only on their current feelings and the impact these feelings are having on them.

If you join a support group and talk about your experience with others, this can help you create a narrative about the trauma and connect the dots - you start to piece together a difficult past with the present, and you start to make sense of your feelings. The key, though, is to **do this with people who are non-judgmental and that you feel safe with**.

If you feel the need to unburden instead of keeping things to yourself, putting feelings into words has been shown to be helpful. A study by the University of California at Los Angeles suggests that, when we talk about our emotions, this can lead to a diminished response of the amygdala when we're faced with something distressing. The amygdala is a brain region that is involved in the processing of emotional responses, among other factors. Talking about your negative feelings has an impact on the brain, and the mechanisms underlying this can result in you coping better with negative emotional experiences.[72]

Let's say you were harassed while walking in your neighbourhood one evening and this made you fear for your safety. After this incident, you began feeling afraid to leave the house. Talking about your experience with others - such as in a support group or with a trained professional - can be key in untangling the difficult event and understanding it better, and the implications it's had on you. The more you talk about this, the more this can help you manage and feel better next time you venture outside.

#2 Re-assess the relationships that deserve priority seats to your life

In our day-to-day lives, we may yearn for closeness to others. We may yearn for friendships or romantic relationships. However, it is important to surround ourselves with people who are worthwhile and want the best for us. This is key in our daily lives, but even more so if you're facing difficulties.

And what are worthwhile relationships? Worthwhile relationships are those with people who are reliable and trustworthy. This is a great measuring stick to go by to determine whether or not you should keep somebody in your life. As we move through life and time passes, we learn about people and we evolve. Maybe in your youth you were attracted and opened up to certain people. Maybe when you were younger, certain people got 'priority seats' to your life. But as you move through life and acquire experiences, you may start perceiving these same people differently. Maybe you start realizing that you don't have as much in common as you once thought, or you're moving in different directions. Maybe you realize that they have a negative impact on you. Perhaps you'd like to distance yourself from a long-term drinking buddy, for example, because this person encourages you to keep drinking when you'd like to quit; the drinking buddy made you feel happy and less lonely at first, but now you'd like to remake your life.

As you go through life, people move up and down in positions of priority: they may transition from close friends to acquaintances. As life changes, so can our friendships and relationships.

And it is important to know that this is normal, and an important part of our growth. We shouldn't feel bad about that.

Anyone who gets priority access in your life needs to deserve it. This is why people who bring you down should be moved further away from you, metaphorically speaking. This can include limiting the amount of time you spend with such individuals or, in certain instances, cutting them out of your life if they take away from what you currently have.

There's wisdom in realizing when it's time to move friends further away from us or bring them closer. **Life isn't static and neither should our friendships be**.

A few years ago, I was at a gathering and talking with Katie who told me about her high school friend. She said that they used to spend a lot of time together as teenagers: they would go over to each other's houses, go to parties together and spend every lunch together while they were at school. Her friend was often negative and envious towards other people, which was something she didn't like. The friend was a **toxic person**: someone who always had something negative to say. You'd feel *more* - not less drained - after spending time in her presence. But Katie didn't consciously realize all these negative effects until years later when she'd clarified to herself what it is she wanted out of life and relationships. She realized that one thing she needed in her life was being surrounded by people who were positive.

When Katie and her friend both got older and moved away, she told me that she made the decision to place emotional distance between them. Katie began talking to her less often and eventually decided it was time to move on. She realized that the influence from her friend was not a positive one. So she found other people to share her new life stage with. She met a young couple while volunteering at an animal rescue. Whenever Katie chatted with this couple, she felt peaceful rather than drained. And the common purpose - volunteering and doing something for the greater good - that she shared with this couple gave her a sense of community. Katie felt content after spending time with them. She'd found friends who had values similar to hers.

#3 Ask: 'Why is that important to you?'

Maybe you're experiencing relationship difficulties, and you're yearning to bring new people into your life or form a network. Here is a strategy that can help take new connections to a whole new level. To do this, you have to understand what is important to the people you've met: what drives them, what their hopes and fears are.

It's like an iceberg. When we talk to people, we see just the surface-level aspects: their appearance, their tone of voice, their body language. But when you dig deeper through the questions you ask, you reach the body of the iceberg: the information that we don't often share with others, but that is truly meaningful to us. It makes us who we are. All these lie deep beneath the surface. And when we start talking about these things, we begin to feel closer to our conversation partners.

So when you go to a gathering, try to find out about more meaningful aspects: someone's inner world and *why* something is important to this person. For example, if you meet a young man and he tells you about leaving behind the town he grew up in, you could ask: ***Why is that important to you?*** Instead of just listening for the facts, get to know the real person. When you ask, 'Why is that important to you?' in an understanding tone, it allows him to open up and share more intimate details. He might be wanting to move because he doesn't want to live with his parents anymore and wishes to become independent. Or perhaps he's feeling lonely in his current town and wants to go elsewhere: a place with a vibrant community. We can't get to know people until we get at these underlying drivers – their hopes, their fears, their motivations.

#4 Before you dive into what you have to say, consider this

If you'd like to strengthen your connections with people, here is a simple tip you can use anytime you talk to someone who's going through a difficulty.

Maybe you're at work or having coffee with a friend, and the person in front of you has told you about a personal hardship, but this story reminds you of something similar that's happened to you. You can't wait to share it. As soon as the other person stops talking, you eagerly start recounting your own very similar experience: maybe it was the time you *also* found out you were being cheated on just like your friend, or the time you were mugged. And sometimes people do this because they believe it helps them to bond better with the people they're talking to. But this isn't so. And why is that?

While it's true that many of us go through similar experiences in life – we start new jobs, experience break-ups and divorces, experience loss – when people start telling you about personal difficulties, and you're quick to add, 'I know what you mean' and then proceed to talk about a similar experience that's happened to *you*, this makes others feel unheard. You might think you are showing empathy, but it doesn't feel like that on the receiving end. Just because something similar has happened to you doesn't mean that you know how the people you're talking to are feeling. Your experience isn't theirs and, as such, you don't know what it's like to be them and feel the way they do. People feel heard when you just listen and take their story in. Allow it to settle in your mind and experience the journey they're taking you on.

When I was in elementary school, one of my teachers,

Mr. Matthews, told us a simple expression that has stuck with me to this day: 'You can't know another person until you walk in that person's shoes.' Just because you went through something similar, such as a break-up, doesn't mean that you experienced it in the way that your friend has.

#5 Take risks and open up

If you have been hurt by people in the past or let down by friends, it is natural to feel cautious with new people. Many people feel on guard when meeting others for the first time. You might be careful about what you're saying, sticking to predominantly superficial topics and opinions. It can be wise to be measured with people you don't know, but it can also help to take risks – especially if you really want to get to know the person in front of you. When you open up and start sharing about a memory from childhood, a souvenir you collected and its significance for you, and topics that reveal just a little more about you, others start sharing too. The more you let your guard down, the more others will as well. They start to feel a kinship with you and understand who you truly are at your core.

> When you take risks and open up,
> others start paying attention.

It's about giving others a glimpse into your life: your tastes, the kind of food you like to eat, whether or not you have a pet. Anything that allows people to learn about you a little more. And this is important in the context of forming new relationships.

You can also do this online: practise opening up a little more with close friends or loved ones – with individuals you consider trustworthy. Perhaps you haven't seen certain people in a while and miss their presence, but thankfully technology now connects us all. See if you can re-kindle a friendship with someone you used to enjoy spending time with. Start a private conversation online: tell this person about what you've been up to since you've last met, share a few pictures you recently took, and ask how your friend is doing. Send along a picture of that coffee shop you both used to go to. This is a positive way to use social media, and you're actively engaging with it (which is better for our wellbeing) rather than passively scrolling. All too often, we interpret other people's silence online as an indication that they've moved on with their lives, and that they're no longer interested in speaking with us. But what if you didn't make this assumption? What steps would you take?

When we take risks to open up, this can help bonds to strengthen.

We've seen that experiencing a traumatic event can get in the way of our relationships, and it can make us feel lonely. Take a look at a letter I received from a student. In our coaching sessions, she told me about her struggles which arose because of a difficult childhood marked by episodes of bullying; the anxiety she experienced made it hard for her to form social connections. She felt lonely, but longed for the companionship of others. When she ran across a friend and practised opening up (even if at first, it was hard for her), this helped her feel better; she faced her fears as Lauren and Bradley did in the previous chapter.

I was feeling pretty alone the other day. It was a beautiful, sunny Saturday afternoon, so I decided to go for a walk around Cambridge and visit a few of the university's colleges. My time here will be ending soon and I thought I would make the most of it. I started off with Emanuel College, it was a beautiful college. As I was walking around, I ran into Daniel. My heart nearly skipped a beat, because I've got this Pavlovian conditioning now. Since I always had anxiety around him before, when I saw him this time, my anxiety welled up in me again. All I could think was 'Keep it together and don't let your anxiety show. Just BE yourself.' We exchanged a few words, I smiled and was pleased with myself for keeping it together.

Then I walked over to the bridge by Clare College - my favourite spot - and I just stood there, looking out over the river Cam. I remember thinking, 'God, this is such a beautiful day.' I loved being there, looking out onto the beautiful old colleges, the river with the punts in front of me, and the rays of the sun fading in front of my face. I felt a deep sense of loneliness and longing at that point. I remember praying to God and just wishing I could find a friend or at least not feel so lonely.

It was like my longing radiated out to the universe, because moments later, this girl I had met at the Christmas formal at Clare College (Stephanie) stopped to say hello. We were both happy to see each other. She asked me what I was doing and I said I was touring the colleges, but that sadly I couldn't get into Trinity College because I had forgotten my student card at home. She goes to Trinity and said that she could take me in - I said yes! So we were chatting and wandered around Trinity and hung out for over an hour. It was great. I practised opening up and telling her about a couple of movies I'd seen lately, my thoughts on the courses I was taking. I felt happy again, like I was full of whatever I needed to be filled up with. The loneliness and longing for the companionship of others were gone-I felt balanced and restored again. My sadness left. We chatted and chatted, and although I had moments of feeling tense and stressed, my anxiety didn't show and I was happy about that too. Practising opening up really helped me and it brought me out of my shell. I'm meeting with Stephanie again in a week and I'm looking forward to making new friends again. The bullying from the past made it hard for me to open up, but the more I face my fears and talk to people and allow them to see the real me, the more I am able to heal.

#6 Forming positive relationships with other people starts with forming a positive relationship with yourself

A client I coach used to be very self-critical; she had a difficult upbringing and her brothers had been controlling and highly critical of her. Her upbringing had left its scars on her. As an adult, almost every time she talked with someone important to her, whether it was her boss or someone she hoped to impress at a social gathering, afterwards, she would dissect what was said and start blaming herself for perceived mistakes. She would conduct a post-mortem examination of her conversations and always find something to criticize herself about.

If we can let go of beating ourselves up, of saying detrimental words to ourselves, this helps us feel better. The key for the client I coach was to remove all the harsh expectations around the conversations she was having. And to begin to notice the positives - her strengths - and cherish the person that she already is.

Here's an exercise she did and that I recommend: make a list of five characteristics or attributes that you like about yourself. This could be your sense of humour; compassion for other people; honesty and fairness; loyalty; fun-seeking, spontaneous personality–anything! Even if you're not sure, write it down. Spending time noticing the positive qualities you have gives you a feeling of inner strength and helps you to feel whole again. Next to your list, write about a time when that positive quality helped you. This could be when you overcame an obstacle, or when something unpleasant or undesirable happened but you bounced back nonetheless.

When we begin forming a positive relationship with ourselves and start to cherish the person that we are, we feel more able to let other people into our lives. And our bonds with others become strengthened.

What do you like about yourself?	
Write five positive qualities you have. Be spontaneous and write down whatever comes to mind first.	Write about how this quality helped you in the past or at a specific point in time.
1.	
2.	
3.	
4.	
5.	

#7 Learn to lose

Sometimes a relationship doesn't work out and, in spite of our best efforts, we can't get the other person back. Maybe you made a mistake and now regret it. As much as you desperately try to find ways to get through to the other person, the latter won't come back. Or maybe you lost out on an opportunity at work, and someone else you know got that opportunity. This makes you want to vent and perhaps you start harbouring fantasies of revenge – but ultimately, this ends up making you feel worse. **In life, we need to learn to lose**. This can be better for our wellbeing and for our dignity. No matter how much you want the other person back or the opportunity that you didn't get, sometimes the best thing to do is to just let go. Let go of ruminations, or of a relationship that didn't work out. As much as having our desires fulfilled feels good, there's also great value in letting go - and this is key in maintaining your balance in the context of relationships. Learn to lose.

#8 Your bubble of safety

Sometimes people feel anxious to talk to others. When you're in front of certain individuals, they may be loud or intimidating, and it can feel as if they're invading your space. It can feel especially uncomfortable to talk to such people if you've been bullied in the past. And so you withdraw. But it is important to keep in mind that you are in a bubble. We all are and it's an invisible bubble that no one can penetrate. You carry yourself within it. When we meet people, we might feel scared of them - but we have to keep in mind that they're not at liberty to touch us or get right up into our face because of that bubble. And it can make us feel safe, especially when we're trying to get back out there again and mingle with people. Whenever you're feeling on edge in a social situation or at an event, it is worth remembering this. It can help as you take the first steps forward following a difficulty in life.

Remember that you are surrounded by a bubble of safety. We all are. This bubble separates your space from that of others. Keeping this in mind can make us feel more secure as we step out into the world.

Conclusion

Relationships are essential to us. We are social creatures and without meaningful social connection, we can become lonely and depressed. If we take the time to nurture positive relationships with other people, our wellbeing gets boosted. Key to this is building a secure, strong relationship with yourself and ***learning to take refuge in your own personality***. If you're feeling insecure and there's no one around to lean on, learn to take refuge in your own personality. Learn to use this as a shelter against the storms, blistering winds and anything that might be going on in the outside world. This is about learning to love yourself the way you are and learning to trust and lean on your inner strengths in the midst of chaos.

If we have momentarily fallen down in life, keeping these strategies in mind can also help us feel like we are strong enough to get back up again.

CHAPTER 6

RESILIENCE & GROWTH: THE SCIENCE BEHIND THIS

In the first part of this chapter, we will look at resilience, which is the ability to recover from challenges in life and move forward. If you have been through trauma, this might sound impossible right now, but there are steps you can take to help you bounce back. Then in the second part of the chapter, we will look at self-affirmations. When one area of your life isn't going so well, how can you make up for that? How can you still feel good about yourself? Through affirmations, we find out how.

WHAT IS RESILIENCE?

Resilience is the ability to cope or deal effectively when you're dealt a blow; you can withstand adversity and adapt to challenging periods.[73] Even though you face difficulties that could lead to a serious downward spiral, somehow you manage to bounce back.

It is valuable to study the people who faced circumstances of high stress, adversity and hardship, and who showed resilience - in other words, they bounced back. Researchers have been asking themselves, what is contributing to people's resilience when faced with difficulties in life?

I remember many years ago, I came across a paper on this. It was a paper written by Michael Rutter, a psychiatrist and the first person to be appointed professor of child psychiatry in the UK. Michael Rutter had written about young orphans who had been subjected to horrible circumstances in orphanages. You'd think that going through this at such a young age would leave lasting negative impacts on you, which would prevent you from bouncing back. While some children exposed to great difficulties very early on in life do indeed remain affected (they have problems with social functioning and inattention, among others), a number of them are able to overcome this. In the 1990s, the orphans that were the focus of Michael Rutter's work ended up being adopted by parents who could provide them with a safe environment. Michael Rutter followed up 165 of these children over time to track their outcomes. He found that, despite experiencing early extreme deprivation, a number of them improved.[74] This points to the resilience of the human spirit. I remember reading this study many years ago, and finding it fascinating and hopeful.

What offers resilience against posttraumatic stress disorder?

Posttraumatic stress disorder is a mental health condition that is caused by something highly stressful or distressing[75]; it's caused by a traumatic experience.[76] However, according to science, most of the people who experience a traumatic event don't develop posttraumatic stress disorder.

There are key internal factors - factors that reside within us - that may offer resilience against posttraumatic stress disorder. And it is often such factors that determine whether someone is able to manage and keep going, or not manage so well, when faced with turmoil. These factors include[76]:

- Self-esteem
- Making room for humour in your life
- Insight
- Independence

This takes me back to my friend Gale. Ever since I've known her – no matter what she's been through in life, including losing her partner and high job stress – she finds time to laugh. And she relies on herself. When her partner of seven years died, she was devastated and cried during moments of sadness. But sometimes, when she would meet up with us and someone would say a funny joke, she allowed herself to laugh. She embraced humour. She showed this purity and honesty in her emotions: she cried at low points and engaged in genuine belly-ripping laughter at others. Gale took control of her life in a way that inspired those around her. And each time life dealt her a blow, she would fall down, but then in her own way, would get back up and continue walking.

Teaching ourselves to not suffer

Here is something else to reflect on in the context of resilience or bouncing back after tough times. My mother, who has end-stage cancer, has told me that we should find ways to restrain ourselves from suffering too much after encountering difficulties, because as she says, 'I am convinced that suffering can damage health.' Her cancer returned a few years ago and I remember how much I used to suffer – on the bus, on the way home, wherever I was, that was all I could remember: the constant pain. Those moments when thoughts of her illness would unwittingly flash through my mind would plunge me into this difficult state that I couldn't get out of. My mother has told me throughout my life that you can teach yourself to not suffer when you go through tough times: that it's all a matter of mindset and how you choose to react to situations. She mentions Daniela, a relative, and often brings her up as an example of resilience: 'Daniela has a lot of self-love. She cares about herself. And as much as she has taken care of other people and given relentlessly to others, she prizes her own wellbeing too, which is important.'

And this is the key. Your own life and wellbeing are important. Suffering does not bring the loved one back or erase the traumatic event from our history. We should trust our bodies' own healing processes and surround ourselves with people who can support us.

SELF-AFFIRMATIONS

In the context of falling down and getting back up again, let's turn to self-affirmations. Perhaps you haven't lost a partner or experienced something truly devastating, but are dealing with various setbacks in life. Maybe someone in your friendship circle or at work sleights you, or you're dealing with a relationship problem. Is there something that you can do to feel better? One of the things you can engage in is self-affirmations.

As we go through life, it is important for us as humans to try to maintain an image of ourselves as good and worthy. And we like to think that we behave in ways that align with our core values. This allows you to feel good about yourself.[77-78]

But if something or someone threatens any area of your life that is important to you, for example, your work life or relationships, then this can be difficult to tolerate on a psychological level.[77-78] Let's say that you cherish your relationship with your partner; so when one of your in-laws insinuates that you're not good enough for your partner, this can feel threatening on a psychological level. Or let's say you derive self-worth from your work; if someone slights or criticizes you at work, this can be distressing. Our psychology is such that, as humans, we try to find ways to minimize the impact of such threats on us. For example, we might become defensive. Or you might start avoiding the source of threat, so spending less time with the people who make you feel bad about yourself, such as those challenging in-laws. But research shows that, something else that we can do when we feel threatened on a psychological level is to use *self-affirmations*. **In those moments when we feel threatened, we can think about the areas of life that are important to us**. We can think about those areas that give meaning to our lives, and these could be: spirituality, work, health and fitness, community, creativity and others.[77]

Self-affirmations can be helpful when the going gets tough. They can provide us with a different and perhaps even renewed perspective on our lives. They can make us realize that sometimes the obstacle isn't as large as we'd thought and that we can turn to other key areas of our lives to feel good. And this can help us get back on life's saddle.

According to research, while the threat takes place in one area of your life (e.g. relationship difficulties), you can self-affirm in a *different* area of life (e.g. health, work, creative pursuits). You could do this by reflecting on the aspects of your life that give you meaning – such as your creativity or volunteering work.[77]

Here's another example: maybe you're feeling run-down at work, and this is causing you stress – this may have a negative impact on the way you see yourself. In order to counter the negative effect of the threat and still see yourself in a positive light, turn your attention to an area of your life that is going well. You might think about your creative pursuits and remind yourself of the piece of art you painted the other night, or you might remember your supportive friendship circle. When we start to think about the areas of our lives that are going well, this helps us to retain a positive image of ourselves. And this gives us the confidence that we can cope even if we're faced with a threat or problem. Self-affirmations place the threat into the context of something much larger: your life, which is composed of many facets that are essential to you. Your perspective broadens and you start to realize that the problem you're faced with is just one small part of your life experience.[77-78]

~~~~~~

The problem you're faced with is just one small part of your life experience.

~~~~~~

When we realize this, we become less defensive about the threat and feel encouraged.[77] Our stress levels become lowered.[77-116] So, if you think you messed up at work or in your personal life, instead of criticizing yourself, turn to self-affirmations instead.

Conclusion

Self-affirmations are something we can turn to anytime we're feeling bad about something or we're faced with a threat. It helps to boost our emotions and this makes it easier to feel okay again.

In the context of trauma, we've seen in this chapter that resilience is possible. Even after difficulties, research shows that people are still able to find a way to keep going, and reading about such work is inspiring. It shows that through the darkness, there is a beacon of light that we can cling onto. And this is something that has helped me in dealing with my own mother's illness.

CHAPTER 7

RESILIENCE & GROWTH: STRATEGIES

When we go through a tough time, our minds try to make sense of it. The internal compass that we've been using to make sense of the world around us may no longer be serving us well. We start reflecting and re-examining our beliefs to try and keep up with the new reality. We may feel shaken and exhausted by this.

The strategies for resilience and growth in this chapter are for anyone who has been through a difficulty, including a traumatic event.

EMERGENCY STRATEGIES

We can grow every day, bit by bit. Here are two quick strategies to help you achieve your goals and grow your own way.

- **Practise reining in your emotions** - especially if they're difficult emotions and you feel that they could harm your wellbeing, such as sadness. When you feel a difficult emotion coming on, notice it and then practise turning your attention to something else that can distract you. For example, watch an episode from a favourite show, meet with a friend and go to a local concert or food market, or take 20 minutes to write about a topic you're interested in.
- **See change as an opportunity instead of a threat**. This can help you to bounce back emotionally and find new things to enjoy in life. An example can be changing jobs: it's an

opportunity to do something that you enjoy more. A simple example is missing the bus: it's an opportunity to walk to your destination instead and get physical activity in.

Write down about any change that might be taking place in your life, whether big or small. Then write down how you can reframe this and see it as an opportunity. What are potential benefits of experiencing the change? It could be moving home, starting a new job, moving school, joining a new sports team.

LONG-TERM STRATEGIES

Use the following strategies if you're faced with a setback or hardship, and are looking to begin the healing journey and grow psychologically.

#1 Affirm the important areas of your life

If you're dealing with a setback, threat or feel stressed, *affirm the values that are important to you in life*. Make a list and reflect on these. Doing this helps to put a distance between you and the problem at hand, as you're expanding your view and thinking about what is valuable to you. It shifts your focus away from the current problem and expands your awareness so that you think about your whole life and what is truly important.[77-78]

Out of the items that you listed, what would be the one key item or aspect that you would place at the very top? Once you identify the most important life aspect or value for you, spend about ten minutes writing about why this aspect is key. You can then select a few more items and write why each is essential in your life. When we do this, we remember that our life isn't just the current setback we're facing; it's composed of many other, meaningful aspects. And this can make us feel better.

When people do this before a stressful task - for example, before giving a stressful presentation in front of an unfriendly audience - just thinking about one of their values and why it's important to them can have positive effects on their stress hormone levels. So you might think about the close bond that you have with one of your friends and the fact that relationships are key for you, or you might think about your fitness goals and how these are fundamental to your life.[77]

When we think about what is important to us, we start to get that sense of adequacy about ourselves again, even when we're going through a rough patch in life. And this is important in the context of getting back up on life's saddle.

#2 Instead of asking, *'Why me?'*, turn the question on its head

Sometimes, when unfair and difficult events befall us we ask ourselves, 'Why did this happen to me?' While reflecting on the causes of incidents can be part of the healing journey, repeatedly asking yourself, 'Why me?' can put you in a helpless spot. And it can plunge you into a downward spiral.

Instead of asking this question, turn it on its head: 'Why *not* me?' Let me try and explain.

I remember a year ago, I took a walk in late evening in the city centre of Cambridge. The air was crisp, there were only a few people on the streets. The dim lights of one of the Cambridge colleges were lighting the path I was on. I came to this tall, great gate that stood out against the night sky, and noticed that at the foot of the gate lay bouquets of flowers; there was also a student's picture and some text below it. This student had died of an illness. He had just entered the second year of his undergraduate degree. In the picture, he looked vibrant, happy. The text described him as someone who had many friends, would volunteer for local causes and had top marks in school. Here, I thought, is someone who has accomplished much in his young life and yet, everything had to come to an abrupt halt. In his second year, he got diagnosed with a serious illness, and after several treatment rounds, the doctors weren't able to control the illness any longer. And he passed away. I remember that in this text that talked about him and what he went through, a line jumped out at me. And it has stayed with me. When he'd get asked by other people about his illness, he'd say, 'Why *not* me?' If other people would bring up the unfairness of the situation to him - for example, having to go through something so difficult at such a young age - he wouldn't join in with them and say, 'Why me?' Instead he'd say, 'Why *not* me?'

When we let go of asking questions such as 'Why me?', this can make it easier to bounce back or cope.

When we try to let go of notions of fairness, it can make it easier to let go of the burden of the event you've experienced or are facing, and keep going through life. When we're not consumed with whether the universe has been just to us, we can keep moving forward.

#3 Create time for moments of joy

Even during difficult times, people also have moments of laughter or positive emotion - and it is important to make time for these moments.

When researchers studied caregivers of people affected by HIV who were in the late stages, they found that the caregivers had moments of positivity.[79] They experienced moments of joy or positivity, such as enjoying a dinner.[80] Our bodies and minds can't stand for constant, continuous suffering. These moments of positive emotion, moments of gratitude, moments of unexpected laughter, can give us some respite from the grief, trauma and suffering.[81]

So make time - even if it's just once a week - for getting together with a close friend for dinner or watching a movie, because this can have a positive impact on your wellbeing.

#4 Complete the Wheel of Life

When I coach people who have been through a tough time and are doing a re-assessment of their lives, I do an exercise with them called the Wheel of Life.[121] This allows them to take stock on where they are now and think about what they would like to do next. It can also help you if you're going through transition or change. Think of it as a moment to pause and reflect.

List five areas of your life that are important to you, that bring meaning or that meet your needs. This can include relationships, health, financial wellbeing, spirituality, creativity and leisure. Now rate yourself on a scale of 1-10 for each life area/domain. A score of 0 represents being highly dissatisfied with that area of life and a score of 10 is highly satisfied.

When you are rating yourself, this allows you to pause for a moment and reflect where you are now on aspects of life that are of value to you.

THE WHEEL OF LIFE

A wheel of life brings to light the areas of life that are important to you. When we pay attention to these areas of life, we tend to feel fulfilled. When one or more of these areas suffer (e.g. we don't pay enough attention to them or we feel like we're lacking in them), we can start to feel like something is missing, such as our balance or fulfilment in life.

The Wheel of Life can give you insights into the areas that you need to tackle to boost your wellbeing.

Please write down five domains or areas of life that are important to you. This could include, for example:

- Money matters
- Work satisfaction
- Physical health
- Mental health
- Creativity
- Relationships with family and friends
- Relationship with a partner
- Free time for hobbies

1. Draw a circle like the one below, and divide the circle into five equal slices, representing the life domains.
2. Label the sections with the corresponding life domains.
3. For each life domain, number the inner circles in ascending order. The centre of the circle receives a 0 and the outermost circle receives a 10. These values represent levels of satisfaction. The number 0 represents 'highly dissatisfied' while 10 is 'highly satisfied'.
4. Think about how satisfied you feel in each life domain and label the corresponding area in the circle with the appropriate number/value.

Here the circle has been divided into 7 domains of life:

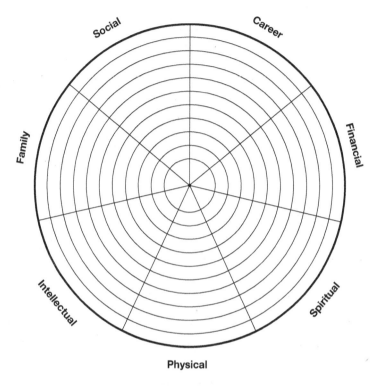

Source: Minimalism. https://minimalism.co/articles/wheel-of-life.

In the following diagram, the very centre of the circle receives a value of 0, while the outermost edge is a 10.

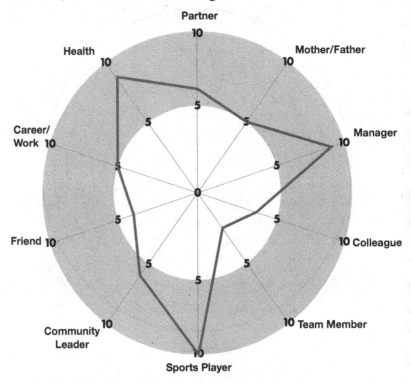

Source: MindTools. https://www.mindtools.com/ak6jd6w/the-wheel-of-life.

5. Next, connect the dots/values (see diagram above). After you have completed this, reflect on whether there are any particularly high or low scores. Can you spot any sharp dips in the outline of your wheel?

In the diagram on the next page, we can see that the social life domain, for example, received a low score (which means a low level of satisfaction) - there is a sharp dip there. The family domain, on the other hand, received a high score.

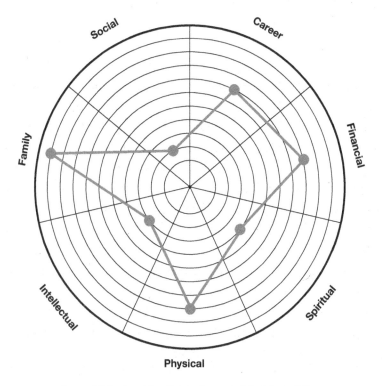

Source: Minimalism. https://minimalism.co/articles/wheel-of-life.

Questions to consider after completing this exercise:

1. What does the shape of your wheel look like? How many sharp dips are you spotting? These signal those areas that need improvement. Take note of what's going on in your wheel.

2. Of the areas with the lowest scores, pick two that you'd like to work on. For these two areas that you picked, what could be the first step you take to improve your score, even just a little? Something that you can do in the next week or month.

3. Make sure these steps are realistic and achievable, then write them down.
4. Take action.

Doing this exercise gives you insight into how balanced and fulfilled you are feeling now. You may score highly on one or two areas of your life – maybe you are doing very well at work or in your running club. But look if there are sharp dips in scores in other domains, such as relationships. Ideally, we want to have 'high scores' across the board, but especially in the areas of our lives that are essential to us. If we don't, we can feel unhappy or discontent, and this exercise helps us to pinpoint where and reflect on why. For example, if you have a score of 3 out of 10 when it comes to your relationships, you can ask yourself: what steps could you take to go up by just one point to a 4? You can do this for any areas with low scores. The wheel can be something you use on a regular basis as a check-in point to see how you're doing and where you can improve.

#5 Tackle the 'worry bully'

Excessive worrying can impede our growth. When we're faced with difficulties, we can fall into a pattern of worrying. We may think that our worrying serves a useful purpose – we're doing something to arrive at a solution for the problem, we're thinking about possible scenarios and a way forward. And without even realizing it, we can start to feel trapped by the worries and rumination. When we have a worry on our mind that won't leave us alone it helps to see it as a 'worry bully'.

Worrying doesn't help us arrive at a better solution. If anything, it makes us feel anxious and stressed, especially if it becomes excessive and uncontrollable. Just knowing this can help us take useful steps forward. Because we know that we can let go of the worrying and we won't fare worse for doing so. In fact, we will fare better. Worries can get in the way of our tranquility and peace. And they can act like bullies - poking at us until we lose our sense of balance in life. But when you start to see your worries as bullies, you stop accepting them and believing that they're helping you reach solutions, as we may think. When you see them as bullies, you're more likely to start resenting them and begin to think of ways that you can get rid of them.

When we have a worry on our mind that won't leave us alone it helps to see it as a worry bully.

Conclusion

Strategies for growth can help people to bounce back when they're faced with difficulties. If you focus on perceiving worries in a way that makes them feel external to you, it can help you take positive steps forward. Completing the Wheel of Life, among other strategies, can help you reflect on where you are right now, in your life, and the steps you need to take to get closer to where you want to be.

CHAPTER 8

OPENNESS: THE SCIENCE BEHIND THIS

This chapter is about noticing possibilities for the future even when your life's journey has taken a detour. The key way to do this is through 'openness'. When people experience something traumatic, their realities may change. Old goals and dreams may no longer be relevant anymore. Old ways of life may need to be modified to accommodate the present reality.[18] This is why, at the start of the Covid pandemic, there was talk of the 'new normal' that we needed to learn to accommodate to.

When our old world crumbles to pieces, we need to tap into our creativity as we mould a new life for ourselves. This involves being able to spot new possibilities for the future. When you're going through trauma, finding your inner strength can help you get through difficulties. Being willing to go down previously unexplored routes is key. Instead of fearing change, we can choose instead to take an inventory of our skills and strengths, and see how we can put these to best use. And we can practise tapping into positive emotion.

Taking all this together, I have found it appropriate to call this chapter 'openness'. Because having an openness to taking new routes and an openness to life is essential, and 'emotion' is a significant part of this.

In this chapter I will touch on two aspects: our emotions and the explanations we give ourselves when bad things happen to us. An important component of getting back on track after hardship and becoming more open is understanding our emotions and learning how to better work with them – this is the focus of the first section. The second section of this chapter focuses on something closely tied to emotions: the explanations we tell ourselves when something bad happens. We will look at the explanations that are harmful for us, and the ones we should be going for in terms of bouncing back and opening ourselves up to new possibilities in life.

POSITIVE EMOTIONS

Positive emotions can lead to our flourishing and help us enhance our wellbeing. Examples of positive emotions include joy, interest and love, among others.[82] You might feel the positive emotion of love when one of your relatives checks in on you, or you might feel interest when you're reading a gripping novel.

Positive emotions have been linked to resilience and life satisfaction.[83]

Positive emotions can also help you cope better when you're faced with difficulties in life.[79-84] In one study, people who had lost their spouses were interviewed about the relationships they had had with their deceased partners. The researchers examined whether these participants showed positive or negative emotions while they were talking about their deceased spouse. They found that those participants who showed positive emotion during the interview were more likely to have reduced grief many months later. In contrast, those who showed negative emotion while they talked, were more likely to have increased grief severity and report poorer health later on.[84]

One of the ways you can foster positive emotion is by finding positive meaning in everyday occurrences. And how do you do this? It could be, for example, summoning feelings of appreciation because you're able to have dinner with your family or receive a hug from a child. Harnessing positive emotion can help people feel like they can get back up again, even during low moments of life.[79]

Positive emotions and bouncing back

Much has been theorized and written on the subject of positive emotion, in particular by a professor in psychology at the University of North Carolina at Chapel Hill: Barbara Fredrickson.[85] This section is predominantly based on her work, but also coaching interviews I've had with people over the years.

When we're going through tough times, it helps to brainstorm possibilities for a way going forward. It helps to identify and test out various options for a way out of the problem you're faced with. And this is where emotions can play a key role. *Negative emotions shrink the range of options that we see before us*. Instead of seeing a number of possibilities for a way forward, our attention becomes narrower.[85]

When we're feeling positive, on the other hand, we feel encouraged to explore new ideas and think about possibilities. **We explore and play more**.[85] And play has been shown to have a positive effect on the brain and can help improve our memory. When we're feeling positive, we're also more likely to savour the moment – for example, we allow the good feelings we get from being around family and friends to sink in and we cherish the occasion. All this builds resources within us and helps us become more resilient in the face of difficulty.[79]

Even if you only have periods of time or moments when you are feeling positive emotions, it doesn't matter. While you are experiencing positive emotions, you are helping yourself to discover the strengths that you have and build upon these. And while positive emotions can be transitory, the strengths you're building for yourself tend to be lasting. They can be used again in the future, should you need to use them when you're faced with a challenge.[85]

During the time that you are feeling positive, you are helping to build inner resources for yourself.

Positive emotions help us live longer

Findings from a study on 180 nuns who handwrote their autobiographies when they were on average 22 years old,[86] showed that those who wrote the most positive content lived longer than the rest. The researchers checked the nuns' survival when they were between 75 and 95 years old and found that those who felt higher levels of positive emotion earlier in life had a lower chance of early death later on. Here are two excerpts from the nun autobiographies: the first except is characterized by low positive emotion (not much positive emotion is evident), while the second excerpt is characterized by high positive emotion (lots of positive feelings).

Sister 1 (low positive emotion) *'I was born on September 26, 1909, the eldest of seven children, five girls and two boys . . . My candidate year was spent in the Motherhouse, teaching Chemistry and Second Year Latin at Notre Dame Institute. With God's grace, I intend to do* *my best for our Order, for the spread of religion and for my personal sanctification.'*[86]

Sister 2 (high positive emotion) *'God started my life off well by bestowing upon me a grace of inestimable value . . . The past year which I have spent as a candidate studying at Notre Dame College has been a very happy one. Now I look forward with eager joy to receiving the Holy Habit of Our Lady and to a life of union with Love Divine.'*[86]

One reason why we might be seeing these findings is that positive emotions can boost our immune system. So feeling positive is good for our health and, ultimately, lifespan.

THE EXPLANATIONS WE GIVE OURSELVES

Let's turn our attention to something that is linked with negative emotion. This section is directed at people who tend to blame themselves excessively when something goes wrong in their lives. It's for those who feel that they're always at fault and are highly self-critical, and they tell themselves unhelpful things that can keep them from advancing.

In the context of openness, the theme of this chapter, something that has a substantial effect on us is: the explanations we give ourselves. The ways that we explain things to ourselves when something goes wrong can keep us stuck or help us bounce back and take action.

When something bad happens to us, we often ask why. Why did this happen to *me*? The answers that we give ourselves to the 'why' question can set us on different pathways: either a downward spiral, or a retention of our wellbeing. The answers or explanations we give to the 'why' question may help us remain open to possibilities - or not so much.[87]

Three explanations have been linked to a condition that is one of the most common around the world: depression. And these three types of explanations are called: internal, stable and global.[88] Let's take a look.

Internal explanations

One type of explanation that people give for bad events is the internal explanation. People who believe that bad events happen to them because they're failures (they believe that 'internally', there's something wrong with them, and they're the ones to blame), tend to fare worse. Let's say you worked hard on a report, your boss evaluated it and then you received a poor evaluation on it. Those who use an internal explanation for this bad event might say something like, 'I'm inadequate, this is why I received the negative feedback.' They take it back to themselves and see the circumstance as a reflection of themselves. The reasons for the negative feedback have to do with the *internal*. And so, you end up feeling bad about yourself.[87]

Or take another example: 'I have few friends at work, because nobody likes my personality.' You believe that there's something wrong with you - it's an 'internal flaw'. This can have an impact on your self-esteem.[87]

In contrast: External statements

On the other hand, people who don't use internal explanations for bad events, but instead use external statements, tend to fare better. These are the people who look for reasons to explain the bad events happening to them that have to do with factors *outside* of themselves - they look at the situation or circumstances. When they look for an answer as to what caused the bad event in their lives, they don't point the finger at themselves. They turn it outwards. Here's an example. Let's say your partner was short with you one morning; the way that you might explain this event is that the partner was in a bad mood, because he's going through a stressful time. The bad mood has nothing to do with you or how worthy you are as a human being. It's all to do with what might be happening in your partner's life: the stress that's making him react in this manner. People who use external statements, *externalize* the reason for what's happened.[87] And in this way, you feel better, because you're turning away from self-blame.

Stable explanations for bad events

Another type of explanation that has been linked to spiralling downwards is the stable explanation of bad events. If a negative event has happened to you, you tell yourself that it's going to persist or continue in the long run (it's stable). So if you made a mistake, you believe that the situation won't improve. Going back to the report example, if you received a poor evaluation on your report today, you believe that you are 'doomed' to receive other poor evaluations from your boss in the future. This is a stable explanation for the bad event that's just taken place. The more you believe that you are 'doomed' to be assessed poorly in the future, the more a downcast feeling can linger. So when the time does come for you to write another report at a later time, you feel helpless and discouraged about your chances of success.[87-88]

In contrast: Unstable explanations

If, on the other hand, you tell yourself that you received a poor evaluation this one time - it's a one-off, and you'll do better next time - then you are motivated to try again. The whole thing becomes something transient rather than something chronic or long-lasting. These types of explanations are unstable. You don't believe that the difficulties will persist over time. So any low mood you're feeling in the moment because of the poor evaluation will likely also be transient.[87]

Global explanations for bad events

People who tend to spiral downwards also tend to explain bad things that happen to them in a global way. If they experience an unfortunate incident, they believe that only bad things happen to them *in general*. They don't stick only to the event that's happened: the poor evaluation on this one report, the one time they messed up in a friendship. When you make these massive generalizations, you're more likely to experience feelings of helplessness that can then spread to other areas of your life.[87] So for example, maybe you said something that upset your friend and she doesn't want to talk to you anymore. And as a result, you're caught in a cycle of self-blame. In fact, you start blaming yourself so much that now you believe none of the important relationships in your life will work out: whether it's the relationship with your partner, other close friends or even co-workers.

So something has happened – the upsetting thing you said that's fractured your friendship – and now you take this as evidence that you're doomed to fail in other areas of your life too. These types of explanations ('I'm doomed to fail') can interfere with the actions you take. When you start catastrophizing or focusing on the worst, this can get in the way of you progressing in life. And it can make it very difficult to get back up – not only in small moments of crisis, but also when something truly devastating happens.[87]

In contrast: Specific explanations for bad events

To bounce back, it's better to use specific explanations for bad events. You are not generalizing, rather you are sticking to the specific, unique circumstance you're dealing with. If you messed up something important to you, you might ascribe this to the fatigue and health issues you've been dealing with recently. The reason becomes something very specific: in this case, it's to do with your current health issues. Perhaps you did poorly on a presentation at work because you just transitioned into a new role and, therefore, you're still learning the ropes. The explanation as to why something didn't work out isn't connected to the future or other areas of your life, it's only relevant to the 'now' and what's going on in the now. This localized explanation of events makes it easier to bounce back from difficulties.[87-88]

The explanations can change

We can change our ways of explaining bad events. When we change harmful explanations, we start becoming more open to the world around us and getting better at spotting possibilities – instead of obstacles – along the way.

And why do some people explain things in a global, stable and internal way? Often it has to do with the role models that we had growing up. If we saw one of our parents consistently reacting to bad events in a certain way, we may be more likely to adopt this. The key people in our lives that we spent a lot of time around, whether it's parents, teachers or peers, can have a significant influence on us.

The explanations we give to the 'why' question ('Why did this happen to me?') are important. They can set you on a trajectory to bounce back or spiral downwards.

David consistently used stable, internal and global explanations for the bad events happening to him. Even when things were going well in his life, he would be down, thinking that life wasn't bringing him the happiness he was looking for. Whenever something went wrong, he would tell his family that nothing ever works out for him, and he didn't expect things to change in the future. If someone didn't help him out at one point in time, he'd assume that the other person doesn't like him so he'd attribute it to his internal qualities (he'd think about what was wrong with him). He spoke about being shy and he saw this as an obstacle. If someone didn't act friendly towards him, he would assume that it is because the other person doesn't respect or is mocking him. So he developed this armour to protect himself against life. When he hit a roadblock because his only close friend moved away, he spiraled downwards and no matter what other good things were going on his life, nothing mattered anymore. It was as if he decided that nothing good was ever going to happen to him again.

The problem with the explanations we tell ourselves, is that they start to matter when we hit a difficulty in life, such as a loved one becoming sick, a relationship ending or a redundancy. When everything is going fine and we're dealing with minor setbacks, then the words we use - even if they're negative - might not seem all that important. We know we can bounce back. But when you go through something difficult, then the statements that you make to yourself and other people can have a profound effect. Depression can ensue.

Optimistic vs. pessimistic explanations

Now if you've been using unhelpful explanations for bad events, this isn't about becoming even more self-critical. It's about recognizing the unhelpful roots of our thinking patterns so that we may weaken them.

If you point the finger at yourself and believe that there's something inherently wrong with you that is deep-rooted, this can stand in the way. If you think something didn't work out because you're incompetent and believe that this 'incompetency' is part of who you are, it can set you back. It can make you passive when you're faced with challenges in life.[89]

Global, stable and external explanations for bad events (the harmful explanations) have been linked to pessimism. They're pessimistic ways of explaining the things that happen to us.[89]

Expressing negative emotion can have an undeniable influence on us. It can have consequences that are far-reaching and long-lasting. A study done on 99 graduates of Harvard University showed that people who tended to explain negative events in a pessimistic fashion were more likely to have their health negatively affected many years later. The Harvard graduates who were more pessimistic – who explained bad events by looking at stable, global and internal causes – experienced worse health later on in life.[90] Some of the more pessimistic explanations by the Harvard participants included[90]:

- 'I cannot seem to decide firmly on a career . . . this may be an unwillingness to face reality.'
- '(I dislike work because I have) . . . fear of getting in a rut, doing the same thing day after day, year after year.'

Why does negativity affect our health?

Pessimism can lead to passivity – we think we're at the hands of fate and there's nothing we can do about our plight.[89] Or we might believe that we have a chronic deep-rooted issue, and something's wrong with us. We might say to ourselves, 'I didn't hear back from my date, because I'm not good enough.' It becomes a broad generalization.

On the other hand, people who use optimistic explanations (the external, unstable, specific explanations previously described) tend to not make these generalizations. People who have a more optimistic way of explaining open themselves up to possibilities and a wide-open road ahead of them.

How to turn things around

And this is where working with a professional can be helpful. Programs have been developed by scientists at leading institutions that teach people to become more optimistic or use more helpful explanations.

Optimism has been associated with improved problem-solving skills. So if you're faced with a difficult personal situation and you're more optimistic, you may also be more adept at solving it.

I coached a man in his forties, about a year ago. When I met him, he didn't smile during our session, and there was this feeling of heaviness around him. It was like there was a dark cloud applying pressure. We met every two weeks, and each week he focused on the events that got him down. But it wasn't the specific negative experiences that I necessarily took note of; it was that he had a particularly negative way of recounting those stories. He exuded a sense of helplessness; he talked about events, such as not having enough friends or getting into arguments with his wife, as if he had no control over the unlucky life he was living, to use his own words. He believed he was doomed to have more bad luck and that his life wouldn't improve.

We did a few exercises together; I wanted to see if they could help him become more optimistic and hopeful for the future. We practised turning unhelpful explanations into more helpful ones. Also, instead of repeatedly looking to the past and being passive about his life, I wondered if he could start thinking about future possibilities. He completed the Wheel of Life exercise (see chapter 7). This helped him to start thinking about the domains that were important to him, and the steps that he would have to take to feel happier and more satisfied in those areas. He visualized how he would feel if he were to change the way he explains things to himself, and also achieve his long-term aims. We also used some of the strategies in the next chapter and, within a few months, the changes were noticeable. He became more energized, he started looking towards a hopeful future in which there were possibilities and his mood lifted. He became more open to life, and whenever the old unhelpful ways of explaining things crept up, he caught himself. He took notice and used the power of self-awareness to change his path in life.

Notice rather than interpret. When we catch ourselves saying or doing something we don't like and just take notice, instead of engaging in self-criticism, it opens us up to understanding ourselves better. This is the first step on the path to change and adopting more helpful patterns.

If you've experienced a trauma, perhaps all you want to do is to be alone for a while and simply just *be* without thinking about anything else. For this reason, I suggest you be gentle with yourself as you take steps forward. Give yourself the time needed to heal, and when you feel ready to take the next step forward, I would encourage you to think about some of the concepts in this chapter:

- How might you use different language as you talk about the difficult incident you've been through?
- How might you bring more positive emotion into your life?
- Can you be open to new possibilities? Possibilities for the future and perhaps a new way ahead?

Conclusion

In this chapter, we've seen the value of positive emotion when it comes to our mental healh. We've seen that the explanations we give ourselves for bad events that happen to us have power - they may influence the way we perceive our path going forward, the possibilities we grab onto and our wellbeing. The next chapter will focus on strategies for openness, becoming more open to life and unleashing your inner potential.

CHAPTER 9

OPENNESS: STRATEGIES

If you've gone through a tough time and are looking for ways to become open to possibilities again, this is the chapter for you. Here, we look at strategies for overcoming setbacks and 'bouncing back', whether it's in your personal or professional life. Here are key strategies that can help you, both right now, and in the long-term.

EMERGENCY STRATEGIES

When people go through difficulties and trauma, they often look for ways to make it through, boost their emotions, and open themselves up to the world again. Here are strategies to do this.

- Research on caregivers tending to their partners who had HIV,[80] shows that no matter how tough life gets, we can still make room for positive emotion. And positive emotions help us get through hardship. All of us go through difficulties, and the search for ways to bounce back is universal. These steps show you how you can bring positive emotion into your life now, and start regaining control:
- – **Use problem-focused coping**: this means thinking about the kind of information that you need and making a plan to tackle your current difficulty (you're focusing on the problem at hand). This gives you a sense of personal control even

when the circumstances are dire. In the research on participants with HIV, the caregivers learned how to administer IVs to their partners, and this gave them a sense of achievement. They knew they couldn't stop the disease, but they could do something to help their partners.[80]

So move away from the negative explanations we talked about in the previous chapter, and think about ways that you can use problem-focused coping instead – the steps that you can take to tackle your problem: this could be making a medical appointment, preparing a list of things to do, or thinking about the kind of support you might need.

- **'Infuse' regular situations with positive meaning**.[80] Participants caring for partners with HIV turned everyday events into small bright moments of appreciation – for example, noticing a beautiful flower at a flower stand. Even if you're going through incredibly stressful times, when you 'infuse' regular situations with positive meaning, this not only gives you a psychological break from the suffering, but it can have a positive impact on your self-esteem.[80] So take time to notice and cherish the small moments of happiness in your life.

• **Learn to reconnect with your body**.[42] When people go through trauma, they may have difficulty recognizing and accepting feelings; their bodies may feel foreign. When you feel like you're losing your balance and are overwhelmed by a particular emotion: just *hold the feeling* coursing through you and connect with it. Pause everything you're doing. Think about where you're experiencing the feeling and just stay with it for a moment. This is highlighted by research from Queensland University of Technology, and a strategy used by participants who experienced childhood sexual abuse.[42] After you've held the feeling or emotion, gently let it go.

- **Make time for play to enhance positive emotions**. No matter the age, when you get together with friends over a board game or charades, this allows you to let your guard down and can help you feel better, too.

LONG-TERM STRATEGIES

Use the following strategies to become more open to the world around you and find a new way forward. It all starts with showing mercy towards yourself - this helps you bounce back from challenges and opens you up to healing.

#1 Be merciful towards yourself

As we've seen in the previous chapter, the way we talk to ourselves can have a substantial impact on us. But so does the way we treat ourselves. When you treat yourself well, other people tend to do the same. Treating yourself well starts with developing a merciful attitude towards yourself. If you make a mistake, you don't beat yourself up over it, and instead of using unhelpful explanations for what's happened (e.g. 'I'm a failure'), you let it go. This is also part of staying open to life and allowing experiences to shape you, and seeing perceived errors as learning opportunities.

A man who came to my practice for coaching told me that he is very harsh with himself: he needs to be the perfect friend, the perfect spouse, the brilliant colleague. He told me about his hair, which needs to look 'perfect' every time he goes out. Or if his face breaks out slightly, this stresses him out if he knows that he needs to meet up with people. He finds this constant striving for perfection tiresome and stressful. But this perfectionism is born out of a lack of mercy towards the self. He fears peoples' criticism or rejection. Really, though, he is the one being harsh with himself.

When we become more merciful towards ourselves and start using more helpful explanations for bad things that come our way (as we've seen in the previous chapter), perceived flaws also don't seem such a big deal anymore. If you make a mistake, you feel that you can recover. By being kind to yourself, you also start to develop an attitude such that other people should be kind to you in return. This is beneficial for your wellbeing, and also helps you bounce back in life after something challenging has happened. For example, if something has gone wrong at work, then if you have this mercy for yourself, you realize that mistakes do happen. And if your boss reacts harshly, you may be less likely to judge yourself. Why is your boss reacting so harshly, as you're only human - you might ask yourself. And this often allows you to see things more objectively. All this is part of remaining open to the ebb and flow of life, with its ups and downs - while being compassionate with yourself.

#2 Increase your tolerance of uncertainty

Do you hate uncertainty? You are not alone in that. Trying to control all the uncertainty in life can be exhausting and ultimately futile. Will there ever be a point at which you've received the validation you may need from your boss, your friends or partner, so that you can now say, 'I am satisfied and confident about my place in this world'? Perhaps you keep trying to reach this elusive endpoint - trying harder to please others so that you feel more confident that they like you. Or you try to find the certainty that, tonight, you won't have another restless, sleepless night, or that the anxiety won't show up tomorrow. You want it to be a sure thing, but the more you ruminate, the more you wind up in a vicious cycle of worry and rumination. **Sometimes, the more we try to feel certain, we**

realize that this endpoint of 'certainty' doesn't actually exist. It never existed; it was all a figment of our imagination, which can play tricks on us.

What I'm talking about is a relentless chase for certainty - the 'needing to know *now*', even though the situation might be ambiguous, still to be determined or beyond your control. This can make you feel stressed.

Maybe you find it difficult to tolerate one uncertain situation; slowly you start finding other situations uncomfortable. Maybe this spirals into compulsions. Perhaps this spirals into superstitions. In fact, over a fifth of people in parts of the world are either very or somewhat superstitious.[91] **Indulging in superstitions can give you a feeling of control when you're wading through uncertain waters** or when you're faced with new realities of life (e.g. starting a new job, waiting to hear the outcome of your medical results, dealing with financial problems). When you're faced with a threat or difficulty, you might feel the need to relieve some of that anxiety. And so you may start engaging in superstitions - for example, 'If I don't count to four when I enter my home, then my situation will get worse.' You may get a false sense of comfort from such behaviour. However, the danger is that the more you do it, the more it can spiral out of control. And it can have a negative impact on your peace of mind.

So when it comes to *tolerance of uncertainty* - you can either increase the *certainty*, which, as we've seen, doesn't always work and can stress you out. The alternative is to increase your *tolerance*: become more tolerant of an uncertain present or future, of not knowing the answers right away. This is all part of remaining open to life, remaining open to uncertainty, and learning to co-exist with it. It's part of allowing the dynamism of life to take place.

#3 The taste for something comes after you start eating it
Here is a strategy that can give a boost to your emotions. When you experience a difficulty, you may lose pleasure or interest in various activities. Or you may not feel motivation to do something anymore. If the idea of starting something new, such as retraining in a new career or taking up a new hobby, feels like too much, then taking the first bite can be a helpful step.

Have you noticed how, when you're not hungry, sometimes once you start eating the hunger comes? And you might even start enjoying your meal? The same idea goes for anything else you may be struggling to start but don't have the motivation to do. Even if you're down in the dumps or are experiencing negative emotions, just 'taking a few bites' can trigger some of that motivation, and it can become easier to continue. For example, say you're having problems at home and this is taking away your motivation to tackle your to-do list. When you're at work, you don't feel like starting your report because you're upset. You want to get going, but don't know how. If you have this saying in the back of your mind, the displeasure can begin to slowly fade away as you take the first step forward. And then the second step becomes easier, and then the third. And you notice that your mood starts to lift. It's all about getting back into motion, however you can - even if it's a clumsy attempt or you feel wobbly along the way. Just take the first bite, and you'll notice as you keep going, that the hunger comes. Or at least, the situation seems more manageable.

A way to bounce back is to simply 'take a bite again'.

#4 Learn vicariously

When we have difficult emotions, it helps to turn to role models to lift us from the low point in life. A positive role model can give us hope that a new path is possible. You may wish to try joining a support group, or finding a role model who has gone through what you're experiencing; these people can shine a light on a new path for you to try. We can then learn new behaviours from these individuals.[92] So this strategy is about spending time with people who are modelling behaviours you'd like to take up.

Self-belief can be increased through vicarious learning. When we see individuals doing what we want to do or who have stopped engaging in bad habits we'd like to give up, and we spend time around them, they become a role model of success for us. And this can be motivating.

For example, if some of the setbacks you've been struggling with have to do with unhealthy habits, such as smoking or drinking, that you've been using to cope with life's difficulties, then spend time with people who have already quit smoking or drinking, perhaps in a support group. This will help you with your own quitting efforts. You might learn about treatment facilities they have been to, or thinking patterns they developed to help them overcome the issue.[92]

If you are trying to find a new direction in life, spend time with people who are open to taking new paths, or who use optimistic explanations when things don't work out. You might have found these people already - you notice that when you're around them, you feel a little more upbeat or hopeful about the future. But you can also find inspirational individuals through joining new clubs, such as a choir or dancing club, or when you travel. Our role models transmit knowledge to us, and we can learn new skills from them.

In life, we tend to have a limited range of remedies or options that we turn to for problems or issues we may be struggling with. Just as people tend to behave, talk or react in habitual ways, they also tend to go back to the same set of remedies or options for problems – even if some of these have proven to be ineffective. We might go down familiar roads even if our own evidence from the past has shown that these haven't got us where we wanted to be. Role models and support groups can help you to break free from this and show a new way forward. Coming into contact with new people can give us ideas and inspiration, and make us feel supported in our wellbeing journey.

#5 Review how you successfully solved problems in the past

If you're dealing with a problem now, something that can help you move past it is to think about how you've solved problems in the past. Carefully examine the steps you took previously to successfully solve other issues. What coping strategies did you use? Review those experiences. Even if you believe that you haven't had many successful experiences in the past, reflect on the positive occurrences that *have* taken place. Write about a time when you overcame a problem. It doesn't have to be related to the key issue on your mind. It could be when you found a flat to rent even though it was difficult to find housing, helped a friend or healed a rift. Here are some questions to think about:

What did you do then that you could repeat now? How did you decide on these steps? Did you start by brainstorming a list of solutions? What strengths did you use to overcome the problem from the past that you could bring to this situation? It could be your ability to see things from a different perspective, your creativity, perseverance, patience, etc.

Have a go and write down some of these thoughts in this chart or in a notebook:

Beating obstacles in life		
Obstacles in life	How did you bounce back? What did you do?	What personal strengths helped you bounce back?

When you think about the steps you've taken in the past and reflect on how you can apply them to your current situation, this not only gives way to positive emotion, but it increases the chance for positive outcomes to take place again. It also increases your self-confidence and reminds you of what you *can* achieve.

Also, get into the habit of noticing when something goes well! When something positive happens and you take the time to savour and reflect on it, these positive moments can have an impact on your brain. Emotions can be linked to various neurons firing together, and the more we experience certain emotions – such as joy – the more those neural pathways linked to 'positivity' become strengthened.

Conclusion

In this chapter, we've seen that if we learn to tolerate uncertainty and use strategies that not only boost our self-belief but also our emotions, this can make it easier to go through life. We've seen that we can learn how to cope with life's challenges from others and also from ourselves through the strategies we practise. We can increase our 'life' knowledge: we can learn about what works, what doesn't and the steps we can take to let go of unhelpful behaviours. This all helps us to develop an openness to life and what it may offer.

CHAPTER 10

WAKING UP & HOPE: THE SCIENCE BEHIND THIS

This chapter looks at a key aspect when it comes to our journey through this world: hope. Hope is a central aspect of human existence, and especially so in the context of trauma and overcoming difficulties.

Hope can be the bridge between two cliffs: one representing misfortune and the other representing a new life. Hope can give you strength even in the midst of the most terrible circumstances. You start to believe that your situation will improve. It's not a faraway, vague wish that things will be better – it is a firm belief that this will indeed happen. Maybe you've lost a job, but hope keeps you persevering in your search for a new one. Or maybe you and your partner split up and you feel traumatised by this, but something inside of you makes you get back up and put one step in front of the other again: it may feel shaky as you're walking on your own again, but this doesn't stop you from going forward, slowly, allowing yourself to take missteps along the way.

When you're ill, hope can create goals for you: perhaps the focus may not necessarily be on finding a cure, but ensuring that your time from now onwards is filled with happy moments. You may focus on ticking off realistic, but meaningful items on your life's to-do list. For example, you might start re-examining your relationships. Hope serves a useful purpose in this: where bridges have been blown up, you start thinking about how you can mend them. You become hopeful about gaining closure in relationships.

When people have experienced a traumatic event or are at the end of their lives, hope can be a life raft to hold on to.

Hope has been linked to living longer.

Harvard University analysed data from a study on almost 13,000 people, and showed that a greater sense of hope was linked to better physical health and living a longer life. Increased hope was also linked to reduced risk of sleep problems.[93] In this study, the researchers used the following questions to gauge whether people had hope[93]:

- 'It is possible for me to reach goals'
- 'The future seems hopeful to me'
- 'I do expect to get what I really want'
- 'There is use in trying'

Hope can have a number of positive aspects for our health and wellbeing. Interventions, such as hope-based couples counselling, have even been developed.[94] Thinking about how to bring this aspect into your life - whether it's in the context of your relationship or other areas of your life - is important. We are living in a stressful, ever-changing, sometimes chaotic world. The constant stream of bad news and personal difficulties you may be dealing with can get you down. But as we've seen, turning to hope is beneficial. It can help keep us going.

WHAT IS HOPE?

Hope means having an expectation for the future. If you have hope, you believe that you can achieve your vision and you're looking forward in time. You have a desire to reach another state - for example, recovering from an illness or trauma - and you have the belief that you can find a way forward. You perceive the availability of different pathways that can take you there.

Hope has been described as a 'positive motivational state'.[93-95] Even though you may be having feelings of uncertainty, you're relatively sure that the future will be good.[96]

Hope is also linked to goal-seeking. When you think of hope, you also think about the possibilities that may come your way. Having hope can help you create new goals for yourself or redirect your pathway in life.[96-97]

END-OF-LIFE HOPE

Hope at the end of life because of illness can manifest in various ways. If you're sick (which can be traumatic in itself) or someone you know is sick, this section can help you to better understand what the latter might be going through, and how to help this person. We can learn a great deal of wisdom from people who are at the end of their lives. When something traumatic happens to people, they start to understand the world differently - in a more profound way. Let's take a look at what the research says on this - for example, research on people at the end of life. Is there hope left?

I came across a study on people who were seriously ill and at the end of their lives, and these people still showed a sense of hope despite the difficulties they were enduring. The study looked at the factors that gave a sense of hope to these people, and one of these revolved around relationships. It showed that even if your time is limited, if you feel like you are still needed and people are there for you and with you, this can be linked to hope. Having others' reassuring presence next to you and seeing that they're willing to listen attentively, even if you're unwell, can instil a sense of hope. Just touching someone and being close by can make the ill individual feel like a valued human being. The people in this study, and all of us in general, are more than the illness or challenge we are faced with; people at all stages need to be treated with dignity. And this can help foster hope.[98]

At the end of life, hope is also linked to a sense of having aims. However, the aims tend to change as health declines. Having aims can give you purpose, a tomorrow to look forward to - all central aspects of hope. In the study on people at the end of life, the latter had six months or less to live, but despite this, the participants had specific aims related to specific time periods: for example, aims related to tomorrow, or aims having to do with next week or next month. An aim could be having 'a month more to finish my book of poems', or 'a couple of weeks to clean my closets and get my affairs in order' - these were some of the participants' objectives.[98] Having such aims gives you a feeling of a future, even though it's in the very near term. In this study, as people were approaching the end and their condition continued to deteriorate, their focus shifted from the self onto others. For example, they expressed hope that their children would be happy with their spouses.

And finally, when participants had less than a couple of weeks or just days to live, the focus of the aims changed again. The focus shifted from others back to the self again: there was a desire for having serenity in the present moment, as well as 'inner peace and eternal rest'.[98]

It is interesting to note that hope never really leaves the human being. And this in itself can give us hope. It seems that hope is the source of light that can keep us going, even in the toughest of times.

When I was reading this study, one theme really jumped out for me: courage. One participant had 'the guts to continue on, even in impossible circumstances'.[98] Another response was, 'Courage helps me to stare my pain in the face.'[98] When you are dealing with pain or extreme distress and yet you still keep going, this is the epitome of courage. And reading about these people's courage is inspiring. It can make us feel like we can get through whatever obstacles we're dealing with too. When I first started reading this study, I felt deep sadness as I thought about my own mother who is ill. But to my surprise, as I kept reading the research, a feeling of real courage began to flourish within me. It made me realize that death isn't so scary, as we so often think. People are scared to talk about death; we're scared to think about it or what happens to us after we die. But it's inspiring to see how participants in this study still created or had aims for themselves even when they only had months or mere days left to live.

No matter how much or how little time we have left, or what we're grappling with, we can find hope and create an aim for ourselves in life. We can find the courage to *be* and bring serenity into our lives. And a sense of peace.

In fact, serenity was another attribute linked to hope in participants of this study. One of the participants described serenity in such a beautiful manner: 'a purposeful pausing that allowed hope to surface'.[98]

Sometimes we can all do with a purposeful pause.

When the world gets too chaotic and we feel like we're overburdened by problems – whether they're related to our health, family, work and relationships, we can take a purposeful pause. We can stop for a while and allow room for peace – and this can be our purpose in that moment. This can also allow hope to surface within us again.

HOPELESSNESS

Let's take a look at the other side of the coin: hopelessness. Why is a feeling of despair detrimental?

If you're feeling hopeless, you might perceive a dark future ahead. For example, you might say to yourself, 'There's no point in even trying, because things won't improve.' Or you might be telling yourself, it's no big deal if you're feeling this way, because it's not important. However, this isn't so: feeling discouraged and disheartened can have a significant influence on your health and lifespan. This is why we need to pay attention and take care of ourselves when we're feeling below par.

People with little hope who face difficulties in life can also have difficulty believing that they will attain their goals, or identifying routes to reaching their dreams.[99-100] Thus, if there is no hope, if you can't identify possibilities for a way out, this can be difficult to tolerate. It can be difficult to go through life feeling this way. As we've seen, hope can be about a number of aspects: it's not just about finding a way out, it can also be about simply hoping for serenity and tranquillity. If you're yearning for serenity, and there is no possibility of this, it may be hard to endure your current reality.

OUR ASSUMPTIONS

In your day-to-day life, sometimes it may feel as if you're running on a treadmill and never getting anywhere. It may feel as if you have goals, but they never seem reachable and this gets you down. Maybe you wake up feeling defeated and it would be easier to give up what you're aiming for. Because, as you might say to yourself, when have things changed for the better? However, this mindset can keep you stuck and it may affect your health.

But what if we were to turn that around? What if you didn't have these negative assumptions that things won't work out? When you say to yourself, 'There's no point in trying because things won't change', turn it around by asking yourself this question:

How would things be different if you *didn't* have these assumptions?

Often our negative assumptions hold us back and we can't advance in life. I remember a business professor in my undergrad degree who told us in the first class of his course, 'Don't assume anything. Because if you do, you make an ass out of you and me.' And then he took a piece of chalk and wrote the word assume on the blackboard: 'ass', 'u', 'me'. We often forget to *not* assume. We have assumptions and start acting in accordance with them. But how would things be different if we didn't have these assumptions? How might our mindset be different from what it is now?

Imagine you have a train to catch. You know you are bit late and might miss it. If you assume you will miss it, you will probably slow down, lose focus. Instead, stay open to the possibility that you *could* make it. When we assume we won't or it's not going to work out, it stops us from harnessing our inner energy and using it to propel us forward: whether it's this forward momentum as we're on our way to a train station, or forward momentum towards our big goals in life. Assuming the worst also makes us stop looking for options that might help us.

If you're feeling hopeless, there are ways to overcome this. Aaron Beck, a renowned psychiatrist and father of cognitive behaviour therapy, wrote: 'Hopelessness is something that can be changed.'[101]

Even if you feel that you have a bleak outlook on life, this point is only the beginning and, from this day onward, you can make different choices.

TAPPING INTO YOURSELF

So how exactly can we instil a greater sense of hope as we go about our day-to-day lives? Sometimes we might feel as if we don't know who we are or what we want out of life anymore, and we ask other people for reassurance. And even though you might get some reassuring advice in the present moment, tomorrow the low mood is back. And the distinct sense of hopelessness.

When you start to tap into yourself and the resources within you, this can give you hope that you can and will manage. When you give up the chains of self-limiting beliefs and thoughts, this can also give you a renewed sense of possibilities and new aims for the future. And when you take back control with respect to your feelings, you start to sense that you can make a difference in your life. Let's take a look to see how.

Instead of looking to the world for answers, explore within

We often look to the world around us for answers: we look to other people to entertain us or to alleviate boredom. This expectation of the world to provide us with answers or fill the gaps in our lives not only makes us dependant, but we may be tempted to give up the reins. Instead of looking to other people to fill our gaps, we should be looking within ourselves. For example, how can we become a catalyst for our own entertainment when we're bored (instead of waiting for others to entertain us)?

If you want to be happier, ask yourself: how can you become the source that gives birth to specific emotions?

I find this an empowering, energizing concept that brings hope. This puts us in the driver's seat and we start to realize that we can take control of our lives. When you think of this, you realize that it's not up to someone you like to call or a manager at work to send you good feedback to make you feel happier. It's about brainstorming different ways yourself, to be happier or more satisfied: going to that gym class to boost your endorphin levels or starting the clean-up around your house to make your life feel more orderly.

Taking back control – 'I am' versus 'I feel'
This section refers to manageable feelings we may encounter in our day-to-day: for example, mild levels of stress, irritation, fatigue or nervousness. It does *not* refer to conditions or illnesses – this is a different matter altogether.

In the context of day-to-day feelings, the way in which you use words to describe yourself matters. One way to feel more hopeful is to use the phrase 'I am' instead of 'I feel'. Here's an example: instead of saying 'I feel low on energy', you replace this with, 'I am low on energy.' When you say 'I am', you are taking full control over your experience. You're not passing the buck for what you're experiencing to someone or something else. By contrast, when you say, 'I feel tired' – it's as if this feeling has come to you, you are the recipient; there's nothing you can do about it. It can put you in a powerless position.

When we use language that makes us feel in control, we start to think of possibilities that can help us get out of a difficult situation. And when you start to think of possibilities, your outlook often changes. When the outlook changes, hope is born – you feel that your actions can have an effect.

So next time you feel nervous or stressed, focus on the language you use to describe what's going on in your body. Instead of saying, 'I *feel* stressed', rephrase with 'I *am* stressed.' Take back control over your experience. By saying that you *are* stressed, this brings on the realization that one option is to accept this experience, because it's part of you. But if you don't like this way of being, then another option is to change it. You could brainstorm ways to *be* something else that might be more helpful to your wellbeing. Perhaps you decide to go for a walk or do some breathing exercises or mindfulness meditation to bring on the calm. In contrast, when you say to yourself that you *feel* stressed, there's often very little you can do: you feel it, it came over you – and this can stop you from looking for ways to alleviate it.

When we change our language use in this way, it can have a positive impact on us. It puts us back in the driver's seat and we start to believe we're in charge again. Maybe right now, we have a small dark cloud forming over us because we're having a bad day, but the language we use can make things seem even worse, as it may cloud our perceptions – or it can motivate us to look for options. Words have power.

Self-limiting thoughts

Let's dive into some self-analysis. When we understand how we oper-
ate, we are in a position to remove the blockages that prevent us from
being in a hopeful state. One of the things we must gain insight into
are our self-limiting thoughts. Examples of self-limiting thoughts are:
'I can't do math', 'I am not outgoing' or 'I can't present well.' These
kinds of thoughts can limit you. They can become obstacles to your
growth. Once we start to become aware of our self-limiting thoughts,
we can take steps to weaken them.

WAKING UP: THE POWER OF SIMPLICITY

Besides our thought patterns, our emotions are also important, as
we've already seen. Positive emotions can give us a feeling of hope,
while negative emotions can bring us down. Sometimes we get painful emotions and we don't know why they arise. Out of the blue, you
could be feeling this unexplainable sadness or emptiness. Oftentimes,
I have had people confide in me that this happens to them and want
to know what they can do to feel better. In relation to this, I'd like to
share with you a personal, true story that Susie sent in:

> The pattern that some people have is mistaking happiness for joy,
> excitement, feelings of high energy. I remember walking through
> the city one morning. It was a Saturday, I was by the river and
> wooden boats were resting on the water. The day was sunny, the
> sky was blue and a plane had just drawn a smiling face into the sky.
> The serenity of the beautiful day gave you a sense of aliveness. A
> few other people and I were looking up at the sky to see this shape
> the plane had drawn. Usually, when days were so beautiful in the
> past, it would remind me of my unhappiness. It was almost as if the

sun and blue sky were in stark contrast to what I was feeling inside. But then I had a thought: happiness isn't necessarily joy or this energized feeling, or laughter. I'd been searching for happiness for years without finding a permanent source for it. But that morning, I realized that happiness can be calmness or tranquility. Happiness is peace of mind. And that morning, as I was standing in front of the river, I realized that many of us may go through our lives waiting for this energy and joyous feelings to surge through our bodies – and if we don't get that, then we think we're not happy. So you continue pursuing happiness, you try things you read about to become happier. And when it doesn't work, you get down.

But happiness can be more rudimental than that: it can simply be not feeling any pain in your body, and my sister can attest to that. My sister, who's ill, has almost constant pain and suffers from breathlessness and fatigue. When she has days that she's feeling better, her mood lifts. She says to my father and me, 'Be happy you're not dealing with pain. When people are pain-free, they don't realize how lucky they are.'

Happiness can also be feeling at ease and just going for a walk. When we lower the bar, then the expectations for how we should be feeling get lowered too – and paradoxically, this often helps us feel better. And happier. This small realization that day was an insightful moment for me, and from then on, I didn't look back.

As Susie's story shows, aiming for this simplicity can be part of our own journey as we go through life. Sometimes we may create more complications for ourselves: we create expectations of how we should be feeling, and if we fall short, we feel hopeless. But when we go back to the basics in life, happiness and hope start to spring up again. When it comes to our wellness journeys, the 'supreme excellence' is also simplicity.

Some days are worse than the rest, but when we grasp the essence of simplicity and realize that just being able to go for a walk or feeling tranquil is a standard that we could be aiming for (as we saw with the seriously ill study participants who were at the end of their lives), this can make the dark days a little easier to bear. And we may feel the first ray of hope again.

Conclusion

In this chapter, we've seen the importance of hope; no matter how difficult things get, hope is ever-present. Hope can help us to find a way forward or make the most of the time we have. Hope is linked to reduced risk of premature mortality.[93] It's also linked to wellbeing.[93] When you feel a sense of hope, you feel like you can move towards an aim in life, a purpose. Or maybe you get a sense that things can and will be different despite your current problems; you can do something to change the course of things. You gain wings for a better and brighter future: a road to recovery and healing.

CHAPTER 11:

WAKING UP & HOPE: STRATEGIES

We've taken a look at the three stages of **GRO**W and strategies for these. Now, it's time to turn our attention to strategies for **W**aking up - the last part of GROW.

EMERGENCY STRATEGIES

When we fall down in life, we can lose our hope. Here are two easy-to-use strategies to get back up and take the first step on the journey to recovery.

- **Let go of labelling**. Words we use are important, so we should be careful with the language we use even when nobody is listening. How we label or describe ourselves can have a substantial influence on our psyche.

   Negative labelling can make you fall short of living up to your potential. For example, you might say to yourself, 'I'm not smart enough' or 'I'm awkward.' When we apply these negative labels to ourselves, as human beings, our nature is to want to live up to them. We want to prove to ourselves that our behaviour aligns with the *self-limiting label* we have chosen to identify ourselves with. This can limit our progress. The antidote is to let go of this. Realize that calling yourself names or other negative words can become obstacles to your growth.

- **Tap into your creativity to find solutions**. When you harness your creative energies, you start to believe that there is more than one way to solve an issue or find a path forward. *If you're currently faced with a problem, be aware that there is more than one option for it.* While this seems obvious, we often forget this if we're feeling numb or highly stressed or facing various difficulties in life. When we tap into our creativity, this gives us hope and increases the chance that we find a feasible way forward.

This chapter will look at strategies for waking up: in particular, becoming aware of unhelpful thinking patterns. When we let go of unhelpful thinking patterns, we start to make room for hope and start spotting various ways forward for the future.

I've talked to hundreds of people over the years about their mental health and wellbeing, and in this chapter I will outline the most common negative thinking patterns, including the unhelpful things we say to ourselves. We will then look at the strategies that you can use to overcome them. When we let go of these unhelpful thinking patterns, we gain hope that we can get closer to the life we want. And we can move on from trauma.

LONG-TERM STRATEGIES

Use the following strategies to beat toxic thinking, find serenity and peace and wake up to the power of hope.

#1 Give up the desire to 'make things fit'
People can become fixated with a viewpoint, such as, 'I'm not good at relationships' or 'I've got an addictive personality', and look for

confirming evidence that supports this viewpoint. Even if you come across something that contradicts it, you still find a way to 'make it fit'. You might distort the new piece of evidence to support the fixed viewpoint.

So, how do you break this habit? The key here is: we don't need to aim for consistency. Let's say you joined a club - for example, a choir or a running club. You had an unpleasant experience one time, so you've decided to never go back. However, after some time, people have started telling you that the club has changed and, in fact, it's very enjoyable now. But because you promised yourself you would never go back, you don't want to let go of that promise. You don't want to let go of the fixed viewpoint. But we don't need to be consistent and fixed in our feelings about anyone or anything in life. And we don't always need to be consistent about ourselves either, developing fixed viewpoints about who we are. Our personalities are not fixed, they're dynamic.

#2 Move away from emotional reasoning

Do you wonder how you can increase your inner strength and gain a sense of hope again in life? One way is to use your emotions wisely; while emotions can sometimes be helpful, we should be wary about being overly reliant on them. Although emotions can sometimes help you decide which course of action to take, especially if you need to decide quickly, emotions may lead you in the wrong direction. So context matters.

Let me give you an example. You walk down a deserted path late at night and suddenly hear footsteps behind you. The fear that shoots through your body makes you quicken your pace and seek the nearest safe spot. This is when the emotion of fear that you're feeling is helpful: it spurs you to jump into action and do what you can to protect yourself from potential danger. But guiding your life and basing your everyday decisions on emotions may be detrimental.

An example of this is you feeling like your co-worker is gossiping behind your back. You don't have any evidence of this happening and this co-worker has been nothing but kind to you; however, something inside of you is making you feel paranoid. There's no real evidence, just an emotion. It might be because someone betrayed you in the past and the trauma of this is still on your mind. You are on the alert for bad things to happen in your new job. But this emotion of paranoia is harmful to you – you're worried about what the co-worker is saying and you're not able to concentrate on your tasks at work. In this instance, this suspicion about your co-worker is unhelpful, especially in the absence of any evidence. In fact, it could be harming your wellbeing, as well as your chances of success in your new job.

The antidote is to remember that feelings are not facts.

Although our emotions are there to guide us, we have to remember to look at the facts and evidence before us. And ask ourselves: Is this emotion warranted? When we look at the hard data, what does it say? When we weigh up the emotions against the facts, this can help us feel more in charge. And it can give us a sense of objectivity and, therefore, peace of mind. This can help us move forward, in pursuit of our new goals. And not put the new job or new opportunity before us in danger.

Feelings are not facts.

#3 Don't use 'always' and 'never'

Another aspect that can stand in the way of our personal growth and hope for a better future is using terms such as 'always' and 'never'. When we use words like 'always' and 'never', this can be detrimental to our wellbeing and to our relationships with others. For example, you could be having an argument with your partner and you might say: 'You *never* do this.' Going for the extremes can make the other person frustrated and angry, and may cause stress in your relationship. Or you might say to yourself, 'I am *never* good enough' or 'I *always* mess things up.' This can make you feel down and it can be very demotivating to keep going.

So when you fall into this trap, notice when it happens. Show some understanding and compassion towards yourself. You could be speaking in this way for two reasons:

1. You're using this language out of habit, because it's the way one of your parents has communicated with you, and you've unknowingly picked this up too.
2. You have a tendency to focus on the worst. When you think about opportunities for the future, you're using dark-tinted glasses. You might say to yourself, 'I will never find someone to be with' or 'I will never be happy again.' This catastrophising reels in the extreme words.

But when you show compassion towards yourself, the reasons for using extreme language become insignificant. You realize that you can become unstuck from past patterns by being patient with yourself, as you take a new step in a different direction.

#4 Beat toxic thinking

I would like you to make a list of any negative or toxic thinking you might be engaging in. Toxic thinking is apparent when you:

- **Use the words 'if only' and then blame yourself.** For example, 'If only I had listened to my gut, I wouldn't be in this situation.' Or 'If only I had applied myself more, I wouldn't be losing my friend, my house, my job.' *If only* statements create fertile ground for self-criticism (for example: 'I'm so stupid to have done that', 'I will never learn from my mistakes'), which makes you feel bad.
- **Discount the good.** You might focus only on the mistake you made, the important conversation you think you blew – while minimizing your achievements and your positive characteristics. Maybe you're focusing on the nervousness that creeps up in social situations, but discount your kindness. Or you discount your resilience and desire to find a way to get back up even when it's difficult in life.
- **Engage in mind-reading.** You might say, 'She didn't notice me or call me lately. This means she doesn't like me anymore.' You believe you know what's on the other person's mind, even though this individual didn't tell you.

When you believe you know what another person is thinking, this can make you start acting and behaving in specific ways, such as avoiding or acting less friendly towards this person. This, in turn, can have a negative impact on your outcomes in your professional or personal life (especially if the negative thoughts you might be having in relation to the other person don't match what's really going on). And it can have an impact on your own peace of mind. Maybe a friend is more distant lately, not because she doesn't want to spend time with us anymore, but because someone in her family passed away or she's having troubles in her relationship. Whenever you're tempted to mind-read, ask yourself these two questions:

1. Can I **really** be sure that this is what's happening?
2. Is it in my best interest to think this thought?

In this next exercise, write down any toxic thinking you're engaging in. And then notice the effect this is having on you, on your relationships, on your health or mood. Then, I would like you to write down one goal you can aim for as you go through the next week, to address these negative thinking patterns. For example, one of your goals could be: 'changing my self-talk and being less critical with myself when I am feeling stressed'. Be spontaneous and write down whatever comes to mind!

Beat toxic thinking		
Toxic thinking patterns	What effect is this having on you? How does it make you feel when you engage in this?	Write down one goal to work towards for each toxic thinking pattern.
1.		
2.		
3.		
4.		

#5 Create your own space for serenity and peace

Sometimes, the days can feel burdensome and you hope for peace and a sense of serenity. This is especially so if you have experienced trauma, which can be exhausting for the mind and body. In your quest for peace, whether peace of mind or space in a busy life, a key step can be disconnecting from the day-to-day world with its burdens and stresses. A strategy you can use for this is: creating a sanctuary in your mind. This can also give you a sense of grounding and hope that you will feel better.

So create a space in your mind – an oasis of peace. This is a space that you go to whenever you need to escape the world. You might imagine an old, wooden chair by a crackling fire. Take a seat and rest there for a while. And you begin to feel calm. But what kind of calm is it? Whereabouts are you feeling this calm?

Create a sanctuary in your mind that you can retreat to.

One of the people I coach, a woman in her twenties, uses this strategy. She came to me because she had difficulty sleeping caused by the anxiety that was shooting through her body. Together, we tried this exercise. Like an architect, she started by building a foundation. She visualised a space, then bit by bit, she thought about the furniture she would bring into this room, the smell of the room, the atmosphere she wanted to have in there. Whenever she felt anxiety or stress surging through her body, she would go to this sanctuary in her mind, light the fire and rest there for a while. And it helped her feel calmer and gain peace. It helped restore her.

#6 Expose yourself to nature

We know from many studies that being surrounded by nature is really good for our wellbeing and can give you a sense of peace and hope. Research conducted in 2021 by University College London and Imperial College London shows that living near woodlands has significant benefits for young people's mental health. They looked at over 3,000 children and teenagers, and found that higher **exposure to woodland had a positive impact on cognitive development**, and was linked to a reduced risk of emotional and behavioural problems for teens.[104-105]

TAKE A FOREST BATH

Another thing you can do while you're out in nature is to take a 'forest bath'. This practice can give you a sense of healing.

Forest bathing comes from the Japanese expression, *shinrin-yoku*. It means immersing yourself - body and mind - in the forest, as if you were taking a bath. Immersing yourself using your senses. To take a forest bath, you leave your gadgets at home. Then you go to a place that you think you would enjoy in the forest, and you let your senses guide you. You simply let your curiosity take you where it wants to. Be guided by the smells and sights around you. Touch the trees around you, take off your shoes and feel the cold, soft earth beneath the soles of your feet. There are even trained forest therapists to help you do this, but this is something that you can do on your own. At your own pace.[117]

It turns out that it's not just being outdoors that's helpful for us, but also just looking out a window onto natural scenery. In fact, the outdoor visual environment can have a substantial impact on our wellbeing.[106] Roger S. Ulrich, Professor of Architecture at the Center for Healthcare Building Research at Chalmers University of Technology in Sweden, has written about this; he's a frequently cited researcher and the recipient of a number of awards. In a study described by him, a sample of patients who had undergone gall bladder surgery were examined. Twenty-three of these patients were assigned to rooms with windows that overlooked trees. These tree-facing patients were then compared to 23 patients in rooms that faced a brick wall. The recovery records of each of these individuals were then checked and the groups compared. What the findings showed was that the patients with the nature or tree views spent less time in the hospital after the surgery and took fewer doses of certain medications, compared to the brick-facing patients. The nature views seemed to have a 'therapeutic influence' on the first group of participants and helped them in their recovery journey.[106]

When we're looking out the window and see trees, grass, bushes or water, this can instil positive feelings within us and lower our stress levels. It can help us as we go on our healing journey.[106] And it can give us a sense of possibilities again.

If you don't have a window that overlooks nature, just looking at pictures of nature has also been shown to have positive effects. In a study of thirty adults aged 64-79 years, and twenty-six students aged 18-25 who viewed either nature or urban pictures, it was found that viewing pictures of nature improved the executive attention of these participants.[107]

Executive attention is this ability to block out distractions, and is involved in the regulation of our thoughts, among other things.[108]

The latter study showed that looking at pictures of nature instead of urban environments can have a positive influence on executive attention.[107]

Whenever I am in nature, I feel a sense of possibilities again. I think about the steps ahead and my wishes for the future. I go from a myopic view, focusing on today's task, to a much broader life view: thinking about whether I'm happy in the present moment and what I can do to become more satisfied if things aren't going so well. I not only find peace in nature, but also hope.

Forest bathing is not only good for the mind (it's linked to reduced levels of anxiety and depression[109]) but it's also good for the body. Forest bathing can increase natural killer cell activity, so it's got a positive effect on our immune function.[109] Natural killer cells help us fight infection and cancer, therefore being in an environment that is restorative and relaxing is helpful for the promotion of our health.[110]

Forest bathing can also help decrease levels of blood glucose, as research from Japan on 87 people with diabetes has shown.[110] In this study, the participants were taken on a forest walk. They were invited to stretch their muscles for about 10 minutes before going; this helped prep them for the journey ahead. They were also told to do the forest walk or bath at a pace that felt comfortable to them. Some of these participants took part in a 3km walk, which took about half an hour to complete, and others took part in a 6km forest walk, which lasted about an hour.[110] The findings highlighted the beneficial effects of the forest bath on these participants' blood glucose levels. And the authors suggested that the negative ions found in natural environments, such as forests, could be a source for the observed effects on health.[110]

Let's take some pointers from this study and prepare our own forest bath. Here are steps for this:

1. Look up where you want to go and make sure it's not a tick-infested area.
2. Go with a group - stay safe.
3. Before the trip, do some prep exercises: a few squats, a few lunges and stretch out your arms and legs.
4. When you start the forest bath, take it slow and easy - there's no need to rush, just enjoy the sights and sounds around you. Let your senses guide the way.
5. Aim to walk for at least a half hour, at your own pace.

When you take a forest bath, this calms the nervous system and it clears your mind.

Conclusion

When we're in nature, this has a positive impact on our brain and wellbeing. When we take some time out of our week to go on a forest walk, this can be restorative and give us a sense of hope again, and a sense of peace - something that we might not find so easily in today's busy world, but that we, as human beings, still crave. And cherish.

CHAPTER 12:

MAKING LONG-TERM CHANGES

Sometimes bad habits feel large in magnitude, like they're taking over our lives. Other times, we deal with small, annoying habits that are sapping us of our happiness and energy. How can we let go of unwanted habits and form behaviours that get us closer to the life we want? In addition to the strategies you've read about in the previous chapters, the exercises in this section form your long-term plan going forward.

A habit is a way of behaving that occurs on a regular basis, and oftentimes we engage in habits on autopilot without realizing. When we're dealing with tough times, bad habits can make everything even more difficult. They can put a dent in your life and gnaw at your life satisfaction.

Let's take a look at habits in the context of our daily lives and the things we can do to boost our wellbeing and feel more satisfied.

HABITS FOR DAILY LIFE

In our day-to-day lives, it can be difficult to stick to your goals, break unwanted habits or form new helpful habits. This section will show you strategies for sticking to your goals as you go about your daily routine, and surprising ways to help keep you on track.

Focus on the immediate rewards

First, think about the goal you'd like to achieve and clearly define it. Write it down so you have it in front of you: it could be looking for a new home or a new relationship, or getting healthy again by incorporating exercise into your routine.

Something that helps you take steps towards your long-term goal is focusing on the immediate rewards.

Often, we think about distant rewards when we're trying to tackle a goal: the promotion you'll eventually get if you keep working hard every day, the marathon you'll eventually be able to run if you keep training. Thinking about long-term goals can motivate people, but sometimes it can also be discouraging. When you're thinking about your goals, something that can help is focusing on the immediate rewards. The reward may be great, but you may not be perceiving it as such today – it's like a mountain far off in the distance: it may be large in its actual size, but from where you're standing, you may see it as minimized and small. This is why people sometimes give up on their dreams: because they focus only on what's at the end of the road. And from where you're standing, it might be a long journey to get there, which can be demotivating. It might become easier to start zooming in on the negative aspects as you're working towards your goal, for example, focusing on the fatigue of exercising, or the monotony of writing a new CV. So while rewards linked to long-term goals (e.g. the satisfaction you get from reaching a desired fitness level or getting a promotion at work) may indeed be a source of motivation, sometimes keeping our eyes on the prize isn't as easy.

Jeanette had a difficult upbringing and, while growing up, her parents made her feel like she wasn't good enough. Nearing 43 years of age, she wanted to prove to herself that she could do it; that she could stick to her goals and persevere. Jeannette had been feeling somewhat lost in life, and oftentimes needed other people to make decisions for her. Now, she wanted to take steps to change this. She was reaching mid-life and decided that it was time for a new way forward. To start this new journey, she'd make a simple decision and act on it: enroll in an introductory course at her local community college. Even though this course wouldn't have much of an impact on her career or life, it could give her new skills in an area that she wanted to learn more about. It could also be an opportunity to prove to herself that she could persevere in a task - something she'd previously struggled with.

With this one moment of decisiveness and action - enrolling in a course - she would trigger a domino effect that would slowly unchain her from her old life and help her wipe the slate clean: she would take new steps forward.

Jeanette used this strategy (not only focusing on the end goal, but also the immediate rewards - you'll read more about how to do this shortly) to make it easier to stick to working through her course and persevere. Even though she'd had small moments of getting side-tracked, she finished the course and did well in it. Jeanette felt satisfied. She proved to herself that she could set her mind to something and follow through. And even though she had a difficult upbringing and her parents didn't believe in her, *she* could believe in herself. This strategy kept her motivated and on task, and it allowed her to meet her goal.

Here is the research behind the strategy. A researcher at Cornell University found a hack that can help you keep persisting towards your goals. Kaitlin Woolley at Cornell University found that when people focus on the immediate rewards related to their vision, this can make them keep taking action, even though it might be difficult.[111] So instead of keeping your mind focused only on the long-term rewards of your goal (which may not be always obvious), it is beneficial to also take notice of the immediate rewards.[111] The benefits you get while you're involved in the activity *now* - for example, the good feelings you get in the moment while you're working out or the pleasant music that's coming out of your earbuds as you're exercising. The long-term goal might be to develop a strong, toned body, and this is why you're going to the gym. But the way to the destination is paved with many moments that offer quick, immediate rewards - and we often fail to take notice of these. When you're paying attention to the immediate rewards, this can make your in-the-moment experience more fun too.[111] And this can help keep you on track.

Maybe now, you're trying to work hard because you'd like to get good grades or a promotion. The good grades at the end of the course or promotion are the long-term rewards. But you can find immediate rewards to make you feel better while you're working in the moment: this could include snacking on something tasty. Or it could be having this mindful awareness and noticing passages of text that spark interest or curiosity in you as you are working away. Positive feelings, such as interest or curiosity, can then spark motivation and make the experience more enjoyable.

Woolley found that students showed increased persistence on tasks when they experienced immediate benefits while studying. She found that listening to music or eating snacks - the immediate rewards - didn't detract at all from their work. These small indulgences actually helped the students keep going.[111]

This is how Woolley's study unfolded: some of the students were given an assignment to complete and were told the following: 'You can make working on this assignment more fun and enjoyable for yourself. For example, you can use fun coloured pens or pencils, or you can snack while you work. I will also play some background music while you work on this assignment. Please choose quickly and quietly any fun pens, pencils or snacks that you would like to use while you work. I will collect this assignment before the end of the period, so use your time wisely.'[111] The snacks that were made available were healthy snacks, such as fruit snacks and granola bars. These immediate rewards weren't given out depending on how much work the students did on their piece or whether they finished it. They could delay if they wished, and they would still receive these treats or have this pleasant atmosphere created while they were there.[111]

The other students who didn't receive any rewards were told: 'You will complete this assignment independently in class today. I will collect this assignment before the end of the period, so use your time wisely.'[111] They didn't receive any snacks, fun pencils or have relaxing background music played while they worked, as the others did.[111]

The results showed that those students who received immediate rewards tried to work on more problems in their assignment than those who didn't receive rewards.[111]

Focusing on immediate rewards makes you persist more in your tasks.

Those who experienced benefits while working showed increased persistence.[111] This goes to show that when you experience and notice immediate benefits as you're plugging away - for example, deliberately bringing in some fun to your work tasks, such as placing a scented candle next to your workstation or listening to music - can make the journey more pleasant. And it can help keep you on track. Not only this, but focusing on the immediate rewards along the way to your destination is more likely to keep you going than is thinking about the delayed rewards (the benefits you'll reap at the very end when you reach your goal). And you can be deliberate about it and bring in these benefits as you're engaging in an activity - as we've seen, this can be done through music, snacks or a number of other ways. However, these immediate rewards may also be an inherent part of the activity you're pursuing; you just have to take notice of them. The rewards may be the pleasant or relaxed feelings you're experiencing as you're engaging in the activity. And becoming mindfully aware of them is key.

When I became ill because of severe allergies, I found it difficult to cook for myself (and let me tell you, this was an incredibly difficult time for me: waking up every night with hives all over my body for no apparent reason, ending up at the hospital's emergency department on more than one occasion because I couldn't breathe properly and having my face swollen was rather traumatic). I just didn't have the energy to do things for myself and felt drained. But I discovered that if I listened to music shows on the local radio while cooking, preparing meals became more doable and enjoyable. I stopped noticing that I was putting in effort while preparing a soup or making dinner, and was more focused on the light-hearted radio conversations and upbeat music. It gave rise to a sense of joy within me and I'd take notice of it. Sometimes when the cooking was done, I was almost sad to stop the music and the 'fun'.

In life, we often have to do things that are mundane and unexciting, but if we help the situation in some way, this can make a real difference.

Switch from mindlessness to mindfulness

Old patterns can be broken. Just as new tree roots can grow and take hold, old ones can wither away. And how can we contribute to the withering away of old roots? By switching from *mindlessness to mindfulness* - becoming aware of what we're doing in the present moment and being intentional about our next step. Often, we don't pay attention to what we're doing because we're on autopilot. But the minute you start being aware of your actions, things can start to shift. If you're dealing with a tough situation, notice what's going on in your life. Has your schedule fallen to the wayside? When we're faced with problems in life, it's important to take time for ourselves and lick our wounds as long as is necessary. But when we feel able to take steps forward again, let's tap into the power of awareness. Become aware of your patterns - what's going on in your life now? How are you spending your day?

Routine keeps us from falling apart. If you feel like you've lost this in your life, find ways to bring it back. *Switch from mindlessness to mindfulness.* And we can do this for little things in our day, such as our social media habits, becoming aware as to whether we're drinking enough water and staying hydrated, or the way we spend our free time.

Routine keeps us from falling apart.

One of my clients deleted the social media apps on her phone, because she wanted to begin letting go of her scrolling addiction. However, she still allowed herself to check YouTube on her laptop. She found that she would begin her mornings by checking YouTube - this was her routine. She'd prop up her pillow up, turn on the laptop and start watching videos. One morning, right before she was about to start work, she felt this curiosity to check a video and then stopped herself. In that instant, she *purposefully paused* and recognized what she was about to do. She switched from mindlessness to mindfulness. She switched from being on autopilot to consciously becoming aware of her next step. After this small incident, she decided that every time her curiosity to watch something on YouTube would pop up or she felt bored, she would choose not to go online. She consciously made the choice to do anything else but that – for example, get up and do stretches, go outside for a walk or cook a lovely breakfast for herself.

Create plans for the next day, the night before

Another aspect which can be helpful is spelling things out for yourself. You may notice that whenever you set out to do or not do something, you are much more likely to stick with it when you give yourself a clear direction. One of my clients tells herself, 'Tomorrow you will not check emails from 9am to 12pm' to ensure she focuses on her key, important tasks. It gives her a clear road for the following day ahead. When it comes to avoiding or limiting something, establish the night before whether you will engage in it. It also helps to be specific. For example, if you're spending too much time on social media, tell yourself the night before that tomorrow you will spend X amount of time on your preferred platforms, and also decide on the exact times (e.g. 'I will check my social media at lunch, between 12:30–1:00pm and again after work between 5:00pm and 5:30pm'). Imposing limits can make it easier to stick to a restricted period of scrolling. **Spelling it out the night before sets out the way for the next day**, so that when tomorrow comes, *you don't have to make any decisions.* You're simply following through with already established plans.

Say it out loud or write it down. This isn't about creating pressure for yourself; it's about reminding yourself of the way forward that you have chosen, and helping to keep yourself on track.

Reframe as fun instead of work

Something else that can help us in the context of habits is reframing. Reframing is about trying to change the way you're seeing a situation or a potential setback. Instead of seeing an issue with a dark-tinted lens and focusing on the worst, you try to change the way you perceive it. You try to see it in a more positive light. For example, let's say you find out that you need to move away for your job. While this can be difficult to undertake and leave you feeling stressed, thinking about the benefits of moving is reframing. These benefits could include meeting new people, having new places to explore and the opportunity for a fresh start. When you reframe and try to perceive something in a new, more positive light you often start to feel lighter.

You can use the reframing strategy to change how you see the new behaviours you'd like to adopt and turn into habits. When you engage in a volitional act, you can reframe your perception of that act.[112] Our perceptions of the things we do can have an impact on us.

When we choose to engage in a behaviour and we see this as work, this may make the road to change more difficult. It can deplete our inner resources. It can make it more difficult for us to keep feeling in control of ourselves and keep going in pursuit of our goals. On the other hand, if you decide to view the new path as fun, this is more effective.[112] And knowing this is helpful in the context of habit formation. For example, instead of seeing networking with new people as nerve-wracking, see it as a play. You're acting out a part; in fact, everyone there is acting out a part: the sophisticated person, the laid-back jokester, the fun-loving individual. Everyone is putting out a defined package to the world and it corresponds to whatever they want to be seen as. Work out what your role could be, what you'd enjoy 'playing out' and have fun with the part.

Think about the different areas of your life and the roles that you've taken on. How could you make those roles more fun? So that life becomes more enjoyable? This, in itself, can be fuel to feel more energised on this walk of life. It's like the clothes you wear on a daily basis. Instead of wearing the same T-shirts that are comfortable and that you've had for a long time, what outfit could you change into that can give you a boost as you go about your day? Maybe it's the nice sweater that you just bought - maybe, it's time to break that out now. And find a way to enjoy life *now*.

Seeing whatever you want to do as fun is often linked to a sense of vitality and can replenish your inner resources.[112]

Conclusion

Habits are part of our daily lives. We do many things on autopilot. But when the habits are negative or we feel like we can't stop doing them despite our best efforts, our wellbeing can suffer. When trying to unlearn old habits, it helps to take it slow. Take a purposeful pause, think about your next step, and use the strategies in this chapter to help propel you forward. When you start thinking about how you can create new, positive habits, this can help you move in the direction of a freer existence and a more satisfied life.

AFTERWORD

In this book, we have talked about trauma, and how the things that we do can hold us back when we try to move forward. In spite of what you might be going through, research has shown that 'hope is scientifically proven to exist'.[1]

I would like to close this book with a final note.

Whenever you experience a devastating setback or trauma, you often grow. These life experiences are profoundly disturbing, but they can also be a wake-up call that makes you reassess your life priorities. They can help you develop more meaningful relationships with other people and make you invest more in goals that are truly worthwhile.[18]

When we're going through something challenging, even though we're feeling awful, we're actually changing how we see the world and even how we see ourselves. We experience positive emotional and psychological growth. We often start to have a greater appreciation of life and we become aware of new possibilities.[18] Our personal strength increases. Even people who have experienced some of the most challenging life situations, such as those who have been diagnosed with a serious illness or experienced abuse, show this growth despite the difficulties of the circumstances.

Experiencing life problems can be tough to bear and can have a significant impact on your wellbeing. While you try to figure out how to cope in this new broken world in the aftermath of the event, you are also often realizing your strengths.[18] You are realizing that you can make it through even though you might not have thought it possible before. Therefore, if you take the time to meet yourself where you are and let hope carry you through, this may just be the life raft that can take you to a place of healing. And a place of bouncing back.

REFERENCES

1. Remes, O., 'How to Look on the Bright Side of 2020 (Yes, Really)' in *Vogue*, 10 October 2020.
2. Dreman, S., *Coping with the trauma of divorce.* Journal of Traumatic Stress, 1991. 4: p. 113–121.
3. Waysman, M., J. Schwarzwald, and Z. Solomon, *Hardiness: an examination of its relationship with positive and negative long term changes following trauma.* J Trauma Stress, 2001. 14(3): p. 531–48.
4. Kobasa, S.C., *Stressful life events, personality, and health: an inquiry into hardiness.* J Pers Soc Psychol, 1979. 37(1): p. 1–11.
5. Maddi, S.R., *Hardiness: Turning Stressful Circumstances into Resilient Growth,* 2012: Springer Netherlands.
6. The Hardiness Institute, Inc. *The Illinois Bell Telephone Study: How Hardiness began.* Available from: https://www.hardinessinstitute.com/?p=776.
7. UCI, School of Social Ecology. *In Memoriam: Salvatore R. Maddi,* 2020. Available from: https://socialecology.uci.edu/news/memoriam-salvatore-r-maddi.
8. King, L.A., et al., *Resilience-recovery factors in post-traumatic stress disorder among female and male Vietnam veterans: hardiness, postwar social support, and additional stressful life events.* J Pers Soc Psychol, 1998. 74(2): p. 420–34.
9. Bartone, P.T. and S.V. Bowles, *Hardiness Predicts Post-Traumatic Growth and Well-Being in Severely Wounded Servicemen and Their Spouses.* Mil Med, 2021. 186(5-6): p. 500–504.
10. Semel Institute for Neuroscience and Human Behavior. *UCLA Dual Diagnosis Program Information and Admissions,* 2022.

Available from: https://www.semel.ucla.edu/dual-diagnosis-program/News_and_Resources/How_Do_You_Cope#:~:text=Active%20coping%20strategies%20involve%20an,drinking%2C%20sleeping%2C%20isolating).

11. Bartone, P.T. and G.G. Homish, *Influence of hardiness, avoidance coping, and combat exposure on depression in returning war veterans: A moderated-mediation study.* J Affect Disord, 2020. 265: p. 511-518.

12. Lambert, V.A., C.E. Lambert, and H. Yamase, *Psychological hardiness, workplace stress and related stress reduction strategies.* Nurs Health Sci, 2003. 5(2): p. 181-4.

13. Lazarus, R.S. and S. Folkman, *Stress, Appraisal, and Coping.* 1984: Springer Publishing Company.

14. Collins, P.Y., *What is global mental health?* World Psychiatry, 2020. 19(3): p. 265-266.

15. Dweck, C.S. and D.S. Yeager, *Mindsets: A View From Two Eras.* Perspect Psychol Sci, 2019. 14(3): p. 481-496.

16. Maddi, S.R., *Hardiness: The courage to grow from stresses.* The Journal of Positive Psychology, 2006. 1(3): p. 160-168.

17. Cunha, L.F., L.C. Pellanda, and C.T. Reppold, *Positive Psychology and Gratitude Interventions: A Randomized Clinical Trial.* Front Psychol, 2019. 10: p. 584.

18. Tedeschi, R.G. and L.G. Calhoun, *Posttraumatic Growth: Conceptual Foundations and Empirical Evidence.* Psychological Inquiry, 2009. 15(1): p. 1-18.

19. Webster, J.D. and X.C. Deng, *Paths From Trauma to Intrapersonal Strength: Worldview, Posttraumatic Growth, and Wisdom.* Journal of Loss and Trauma, 2015. 20: p. 253-266.

20. Fraser, W. 'Trust Resilience: Engaging and Cultivating Growth'. Washington State Lean Conference. 2021. Available from: https://results.wa.gov/sites/default/files/WendyFraser_Oct28_PRESENTATION%20%281%29.pdf.

21. Sanghee Chun, Y.L., *The experience of posttraumatic growth for people with spinal cord injury.* Qualitative Health Research. 18(7): p. 877–890.

22. Teti, M., et al., *'I Created Something New with Something that Had Died': Photo-Narratives of Positive Transformation Among Women with HIV.* AIDS Behav, 2015. 19(7): p. 1275–87.

23. Siebrecht Vanhooren, M.L., and J. Dezutter, *Posttraumatic growth during incarceration: a case study from an experiential-existential perspective.* Journal of Humanistic Psychology, 2018. 58(2): p. 144–167.

24. Lyon, I., P. Fisher, and F. Gracey, *'Putting a new perspective on life': a qualitative grounded theory of posttraumatic growth following acquired brain injury.* Disabil Rehabil, 2021. 43(22): p. 3225–33.

25. Crawford, J.J., A.M.G., and J. Tracey, *An examination of posttraumatic growth in Canadian and American ParaSport athletes with acquired spinal cord injury.* Psychology of Sport and Exercise, 2014. 15(4): p. 399–406.

26. Carstensen, L.L., D.M. Isaacowitz, and S.T. Charles, *Taking time seriously. A theory of socioemotional selectivity.* Am Psychol, 1999. 54(3): p. 165–81.

27. Fingerman, K.L. and M. Perlmutter, *Future time perspective and life events across adulthood.* J Gen Psychol, 1995. 122(1): p. 95–111.

28. Carstensen, L.L., *Evidence for a life-span theory of socioemotional selectivity.* Current Directions in Psychological Science, 1995. 4(5): p. 151–6.

29. Carstensen, L.L. and B.L. Fredrickson, *Influence of HIV status and age on cognitive representations of others.* Health Psychol, 1998. 17(6): p. 494–503.

30. Büssing, A., et al., *Experience of gratitude, awe and beauty in life among patients with multiple sclerosis and psychiatric disorders.* Health Qual Life Outcomes, 2014. 12: p. 63.

31. Harvard Health Publishing. Harvard Medical School. *Giving thanks can make you happier,* 2021. Available from: https://www.health.harvard.edu/healthbeat/giving-thanks-can-make-you-happier#:~:text=In%20positive%20psychology%20research%2C%20gratitude,adversity%2C%20and%20build%20strong%20relationships.

32. Seligman, M.E., et al., *Positive psychology progress: empirical validation of interventions.* Am Psychol, 2005. 60(5): p. 410-21.

33. Adler, M.G. and N.S. Fagley, *Appreciation: individual differences in finding value and meaning as a unique predictor of subjective well-being.* J Pers, 2005. 73(1): p. 79-114.

34. Stellar, J.E., et al., *Positive affect and markers of inflammation: discrete positive emotions predict lower levels of inflammatory cytokines.* Emotion, 2015. 15(2): p. 129-33.

35. Luo, Y. and S.G. Zheng, *Hall of Fame among Pro-inflammatory Cytokines: Interleukin-6 Gene and Its Transcriptional Regulation Mechanisms.* Front Immunol, 2016. 7: p. 604.

36. Dinarello, C.A., *Proinflammatory cytokines.* Chest, 2000. 118(2): p. 503-8.

37. van Elk, M., et al., *The neural correlates of the awe experience: Reduced default mode network activity during feelings of awe.* Hum Brain Mapp, 2019. 40(12): p. 3561-74.

38. Summer Allen, J.T.F. *The Science of Awe.* 2018. Available from: https://ggsc.berkeley.edu/images/uploads/GGSC-JTF_White_Paper-Awe_FINAL.pdf.

39. New Scientist. *Science with Sam: What is awe?* 2021. Available from: https://www.newscientist.com/article/0-science-with-sam-what-is-awe/.

40. Wood, A.M., et al., *Gratitude influences sleep through the mechanism of pre-sleep cognitions.* J Psychosom Res, 2009. 66(1): p. 43-8.

41. Alkozei, A., et al., *The Association Between Trait Gratitude and Self-Reported Sleep Quality Is Mediated by Depressive Mood State*. Behav Sleep Med, 2019. 17(1): p. 41-8.

42. Vilenica, S., *Pathways to Peace: A phenomenological exploration of the processes of healing and posttraumatic growth following childhood sexual assault*. 2014, Queensland University of Technology.

43. San Francisco State University, *Buying Experiences, Not Possessions, Leads To Greater Happiness*. 2009, Science Daily.

44. Elizabeth W Dunn, D.T.G., Timothy D Wilson, *If money doesn't make you happy, then you probably aren't spending it right*. Journal of Consumer Psychology, 2011. 21(2): p. 115-125.

45. McLeod, S. *Maslow's Hierarchy of Needs*. 2022. Available from: https://www.simplypsychology.org/maslow.html#:~:text=There%20are%20five%20levels%20in,esteem%2C%20and%20self%2Dactualization.

46. Ozbay, F., et al., *Social support and resilience to stress: from neurobiology to clinical practice*. Psychiatry (Edgmont), 2007. 4(5): p. 35-40.

47. Kawachi, I. and L.F. Berkman, *Social ties and mental health*. J Urban Health, 2001. 78(3): p. 458-67.

48. Southwick, S.M., M. Vythilingam, and D.S. Charney, *The psychobiology of depression and resilience to stress: implications for prevention and treatment*. Annu Rev Clin Psychol, 2005. 1: p. 255-91.

49. Ghent, A., *The happiness effect*. Bull World Health Organ, 2011. 89(4): p. 246-7.

50. Vaillant, G.E., *What are the Secrets to a Happy Life?*, in *Greater Good Magazine*. 2013.

51. Miller, M. *What makes a good life? 3 Lessons on Life, Love, and Decision Making from the Harvard Grant Study*. Available from: https://www.6seconds.org/2021/04/19/harvard-grant-study/.

52. Holt-Lunstad, J., *The Potential Public Health Relevance of Social Isolation and Loneliness: Prevalence, Epidemiology, and Risk Factors.* Public Policy & Aging Report, 2017. 27(4): p. 127-130.

53. World Health Organization. *Social Isolation and Loneliness.* 2022. Available from: https://www.who.int/teams/social-determinants-of-health/demographic-change-and-healthy-ageing/social-isolation-and-loneliness.

54. Surkalim, D.L., et al., *The prevalence of loneliness across 113 countries: systematic review and meta-analysis.* Bmj, 2022. 376: p. e067068.

55. Brown-Bowers, A., et al., *Cognitive-behavioral conjoint therapy for posttraumatic stress disorder: application to a couple's shared traumatic experience.* J Clin Psychol, 2012. 68(5): p. 536-47.

56. Craig Haen, Anna Marie Weber. *Beyond retribution: Working through revenge fantasies with traumatized young people.* The Arts in Psychotherapy, 2009. 36(2): p. 84-93.

57. Kaiser, C.R., S.B. Vick, and B. Major, *A prospective investigation of the relationship between just-world beliefs and the desire for revenge after September 11, 2001.* Psychol Sci, 2004. 15(7): p. 503-6.

58. Carlsmith, K.M., T.D. Wilson, and D.T. Gilbert, *The paradoxical consequences of revenge.* J Pers Soc Psychol, 2008. 95(6): p. 1316-24.

59. Bushman, B., *Does Venting Anger Feed or Extinguish the Flame? Catharsis, Rumination, Distraction, Anger, and Aggressive Responding.* Personality and Social Psychology Bulletin, 2002. 28(6): p. 724-731.

60. Bushman, B.J. *School of Communication.* 2022. Available from: https://comm.osu.edu/people/bushman.20.

61. Cheng, C., et al., *Prevalence of social media addiction across 32 nations: Meta-analysis with subgroup analysis of classification schemes and cultural values.* Addict Behav, 2021. 117: p. 106845.

62. Ofcom, *News Consumption in the UK: 2022.* Available from: https://www.ofcom.org.uk/__data/assets/pdf_file/0024/241827/News-Consumption-in-the-UK-Overview-of-findings-2022.pdf *Overview of research findings.*

63. Emily A. Vogels, R.G.-W., Navid Massarat. *Teens, Social Media and Technology 2022.* 2022. Available from: https://www.pewresearch.org/internet/2022/08/10/teens-social-media-and-technology-2022/.

64. Bennett, B.L., et al., *Examining the impact of social media on mood and body dissatisfaction using ecological momentary assessment.* J Am Coll Health, 2020. 68(5): p. 502–508.

65. Odgers, C.L. and M.R. Jensen, *Annual Research Review: Adolescent mental health in the digital age: facts, fears, and future directions.* J Child Psychol Psychiatry, 2020. 61(3): p. 336–348.

66. Zara Abrams, A.P.A. *How can we minimize Instagram's harmful effects?* 2021. Available from: https://www.apa.org/monitor/2022/03/feature-minimize-instagram-effects.

67. Seabrook, E.M., M.L. Kern, and N.S. Rickard, *Social Networking Sites, Depression, and Anxiety: A Systematic Review.* JMIR Ment Health, 2016. 3(4): p. e50.

68. Helmut Appel, J.C., Alexander L. Gerlach, *Social comparison, envy, and depression on Facebook: a study looking at the effects of high comparison standards on depressed individuals.* Journal of Social and Clinical Psychology, 2015. 34(4): p. 277–289.

69. Association for Psychological Science. *Social Media 'Likes' Impact Teens' Brains and Behavior.* 2016. Available from: https://www.psychologicalscience.org/news/releases/social-media-likes-impact-teens-brains-and-behavior.html.

70. Sherman, L.E., et al., *The Power of the Like in Adolescence: Effects of Peer Influence on Neural and Behavioral Responses to Social Media.* Psychol Sci, 2016. 27(7): p. 1027-35.

71. Alutaybi, A., et al., *Combating Fear of Missing Out (FoMO) on Social Media: The FoMO-R Method.* Int J Environ Res Public Health, 2020. 17(17).

72. Lieberman, M.D., et al., *Putting feelings into words: affect labeling disrupts amygdala activity in response to affective stimuli.* Psychol Sci, 2007. 18(5): p. 421-8.

73. American Psychological Association. *Resilience.* 2022. Available from: https://www.apa.org/topics/resilience.

74. Nuffield Foundation. Michael Rutter, Edmund Sonuga-Barke. *English and Romanian Adoptee study – English-Romanian Adoption.* 2022. Available from: https://www.nuffieldfoundation.org/project/english-and-romanian-adoptee-study.

75. National Health Service. *Overview - Post-traumatic stress disorder* 2022. Available from: https://www.nhs.uk/mental-health/conditions/post-traumatic-stress-disorder-ptsd/overview/.

76. Ahmed, A.S., *Post-traumatic stress disorder, resilience and vulnerability.* Advances in Psychiatric Treatment 2007. 13: p. 369-375.

77. Annual Reviews. *A Lecture in Psychology: The Psychology of Change: Self-Affirmation and Social Psychological Intervention.* 2022: Annual Review of Psychology. Available from: https://www.annualreviews.org/do/10.1146/do.multimedia.2013.12.17.238/abs/

78. Cohen, G.L. and D.K. Sherman, *The psychology of change: self-affirmation and social psychological intervention.* Annu Rev Psychol, 2014. 65: p. 333-71.

79. Michele M Tugade, Barbara L. Fredrickson, *Regulation of positive emotions: emotion regulation strategies that promote resilience.* Journal of Happiness Studies, 2007. 8: p. 311-333.

80. Folkman, S., *Positive psychological states and coping with severe stress.* Soc Sci Med, 1997. 45(8): p. 1207-21.
81. Folkman, S. and J.T. Moskowitz, *Positive affect and the other side of coping.* Am Psychol, 2000. 55(6): p. 647-54.
82. Fredrickson, B.L., *The role of positive emotions in positive psychology. The broaden-and-build theory of positive emotions.* Am Psychol, 2001. 56(3): p. 218-26.
83. Cohn, M.A., et al., *Happiness unpacked: positive emotions increase life satisfaction by building resilience.* Emotion, 2009. 9(3): p. 361-8.
84. Bonanno, G.A. and D. Keltner, *Facial expressions of emotion and the course of conjugal bereavement.* J Abnorm Psychol, 1997. 106(1): p. 126-37.
85. Fredrickson, B.L. and C. Branigan, *Positive emotions broaden the scope of attention and thought-action repertoires.* Cogn Emot, 2005. 19(3): p. 313-332.
86. Danner, D.D., D.A. Snowdon, and W.V. Friesen, *Positive emotions in early life and longevity: findings from the nun study.* J Pers Soc Psychol, 2001. 80(5): p. 804-13.
87. Peterson, C. and M.E. Seligman, *Causal explanations as a risk factor for depression: theory and evidence.* Psychol Rev, 1984. 91(3): p. 347-74.
88. The Anxiety and Depression Association of America. *Psychological Models of Depression.* Available from: https://adaa.org/sites/default/files/Tilton405.pdf.
89. Lin, E.H. and C. Peterson, *Pessimistic explanatory style and response to illness.* Behav Res Ther, 1990. 28(3): p. 243-8.
90. Peterson, C., M.E. Seligman, and G.E. Vaillant, *Pessimistic explanatory style is a risk factor for physical illness: a thirty-five-year longitudinal study.* J Pers Soc Psychol, 1988. 55(1): p. 23-7.
91. Ballard, J. *Do Americans really believe Friday the 13th is unlucky?* . 2019; Available from: https://today.yougov.com/topics/soci-

ety/articles-reports/2019/09/13/friday-the-13th-unlucky-poll-survey

92. Elshatarat RA, Y.M., Khraim FM, Saleh ZT, Afaneh TR, *Self-efficacy in treating tobacco use: A review article.* Proceedings of Singapore Healthcare, 2016. 25(4): p. 243-8.

93. Katelyn N.G. Long, E.S.K., Ying Chen, Matthew F.Wilson, Everett L.Worthington Jr, Tyler J.VanderWeele, *The role of Hope in subsequent health and well-being for older adults: An outcome-wide longitudinal approach.* Global Epidemiology, 2020. 2: p. 100041.

94. Ripley, J.S., Leon, C., Worthington, E. L., Jr., Berry, J. W., Davis, E. B., Smith, A., Atkinson, A., & Sierra, T, *Efficacy of religion-accommodative strategic hope-focused theory applied to couples therapy.* Couple and Family Psychology: Research and Practice, 2014. 3(2): p. 83-98.

95. Snyder, C.R. and D.R. Forsyth, *Handbook of Social and Clinical Psychology: The Health Perspective.* 1991: Pergamon Press.

96. Silvia C. Hernandez, J.C.O., *A Systematic Review of Interventions for Hope/Hopelessness in Older Adults.* Clinical Gerontologist, 2021. 44(2): p. 97-111.

97. Chang, E.C.H., *Optimism & Pessimism: Implications for Theory, Research, and Practice.* 2001: American Psychological Association.

98. Herth, K., *Fostering hope in terminally-ill people.* J Adv Nurs, 1990. 15(11): p. 1250-9.

99. Everson, S.A., et al., *Hopelessness and risk of mortality and incidence of myocardial infarction and cancer.* Psychosom Med, 1996. 58(2): p. 113-21.

100. Huen, J.M., et al., *Hope and Hopelessness: The Role of Hope in Buffering the Impact of Hopelessness on Suicidal Ideation.* PLoS One, 2015. 10(6): p. e0130073.

101. Aaron Beck, G.B., Robert Berchick, Bonnie Stewart, Robert Steer, *Relationship between hopelessness and ultimate suicide: a*

replication with psychiatric outpatients. The American Journal of Psychiatry, 1990. 147: p. 190-5.

102. Longfellow, H.W. quote accessed from: https://www.good reads.com/quotes/56831-in-character-in-manner-in-style-in-all-the-things.

103. Longfellow, H.W.; Available from: https://www.hwlongfellow. org/poems_poem.php?pid=39.

104. University College London. *Living near woodlands is good for children and young people's mental health.* 2021. Available from: https://www.ucl.ac.uk/news/2021/jul/living-near-woodlands-good-children-and-young-peoples-mental-health.

105. Maes, M.J.A., Pirani, M., Booth, E.R. et al., *Benefit of woodland and other natural environments for adolescents' cognition and mental health.* Nature Sustainability, 2021. 4: p. 851-858

106. Ulrich, R.S., *View through a window may influence recovery from surgery.* Science, 1984. 224(4647): p. 420-1.

107. Gamble, K.R., J.H. Howard, Jr., and D.V. Howard, *Not just scenery: viewing nature pictures improves executive attention in older adults.* Exp Aging Res, 2014. 40(5): p. 513-30.

108. Rueda, M.R., P. Checa, and L.M. Cómbita, *Enhanced efficiency of the executive attention network after training in preschool children: immediate changes and effects after two months.* Dev Cogn Neurosci, 2012. 2 Suppl 1(Suppl 1): p. S192-204.

109. Li, Q., et al., *Forest bathing enhances human natural killer activity and expression of anti-cancer proteins.* Int J Immunopathol Pharmacol, 2007. 20(2 Suppl 2): p. 3-8.

110. Ohtsuka, Y., N. Yabunaka, and S. Takayama, *Shinrin-yoku (forest-air bathing and walking) effectively decreases blood glucose levels in diabetic patients.* Int J Biometeorol, 1998. 41(3): p. 125-7.

111. Kaitlin Woolley, A.F., *For the Fun of It: Harnessing Immediate Rewards to Increase Persistence in Long-Term Goals.* Journal of Consumer Research, 2016. 42(6).

112. Juliano Laran, C.J., *Work or Fun? How Task Construal and Completion Influence Regulatory Behavior*. Journal of Consumer Research, 2011. 37(6): pp. 967-83.

113. Herman, J.L., *Trauma and Recovery: The Aftermath of Violence—from Domestic Abuse to Political Terror*, 1992: Basic Books, New York.

114. Lafarge L., 'The wish for revenge'. *Psychoanalytic Quarterly*, 2006. 75(2): pp. 447-75

115. Wangh, S., 'Revenge and forgiveness in Laramie, Wyoming'. *Psychoanalytic Dialogues*, 2005. 15(1): pp. 1-16.

116. Creswell, J. D., Welch, W. T., Taylor, S. E., Sherman, D. K., Gruenewald, T. L., & Mann, T. 'Affirmation of Personal Values Buffers Neuroendocrine and Psychological Stress Responses'. *Psychological Science*, 2005. 16(11): pp. 846-51.

117. Li, Q. '"Forest Bathing" Is Great for Your Health. Here's How to Do It'. *Time*, 2018. Available from: https://time.com/5259602/japanese-forest-bathing/.

118. Park, C.L. 'Making sense of the meaning literature: an integrative review of meaning making and its effects on adjustment to stressful life events'. *Psychological Bulletin*, 2010. 136(2) pp. 257-301.

119. Greenberg, D.M., S. Baron-Cohen, N. Rosenberg, P. Fonagy, P.J. Rentfrow. 'Elevated empathy in adults following childhood trauma'. *PLoS One*, 3 Oct 2018. 13(10):e0203886.

120. 'Hopper E. Maslow's hierarchy of needs explained'. 2020. Available from: https://www.thoughtco.com/maslows-hierarchy-of-needs-4582571.

121. 'The Wheel of Life'. Mind Tools Content Team. 2022. Available from: https://www.mindtools.com/ak6jd6w/the-wheel-of-life.

ACKNOWLEDGEMENTS

I would like to thank Marianne Tatepo for believing in me and making the concept for this book a reality. I am truly grateful to my great editor, Ru Merritt, for your dedication and valuable suggestions that have helped shape this book. I am also deeply thankful to Jess Anderson, Editorial Manager at Ebury Publishing - thank you for always being there to support me and encouraging me to take the book in the direction I wished. Ru and Jess - it has been a real pleasure collaborating with both of you, and I have enjoyed every step of the way. I am also grateful to Becky Alexander, the brilliant copyeditor of this book - your insightful comments and edits have helped shape this book, and I am happy we were able to continue our collaboration. I am thrilled to be part of the Happy Place family - Fearne Cotton, I thank you for this. I also loved being at the Happy Place festival and meeting you there last summer. Thank you to everyone who was involved in this book, including Lizzy Gray, Danai Denga, Rachel Johnson, Daniela Mestriner, Katie Cregg and Rachel Johnson. Thank you to Ebury and Penguin Random House.

I am grateful to my parents and grandmother, who provided me with unconditional love and support throughout my whole life. Thank you also to Philipp Seiler for lending a hand whenever I needed it.

I am grateful to the Mind Propulsion Laboratory for his song, 'Still Waiting', which is a concrete example of someone going through trauma and coping with it through artistic expression.

I would like to thank the University of Cambridge for everything: you have paved the way for some of the brightest minds who have made a mark with their research, teaching, and discoveries. I am truly inspired by this institution and am humbled to be part of it. I am incredibly grateful to the people I worked with, including Dr. Louise Lafortune and Professor Carol Brayne, as well as everyone I collaborated with as part of the EPIC-Norfolk study (one of my greatest memories).